Genuine Origami

43 Mathematically-Based Models, From Simple to Complex

Jun Maekawa

JAPAN PUBLICATIONS TRADING CO., LTD.

◈ Fundamental Models ◈

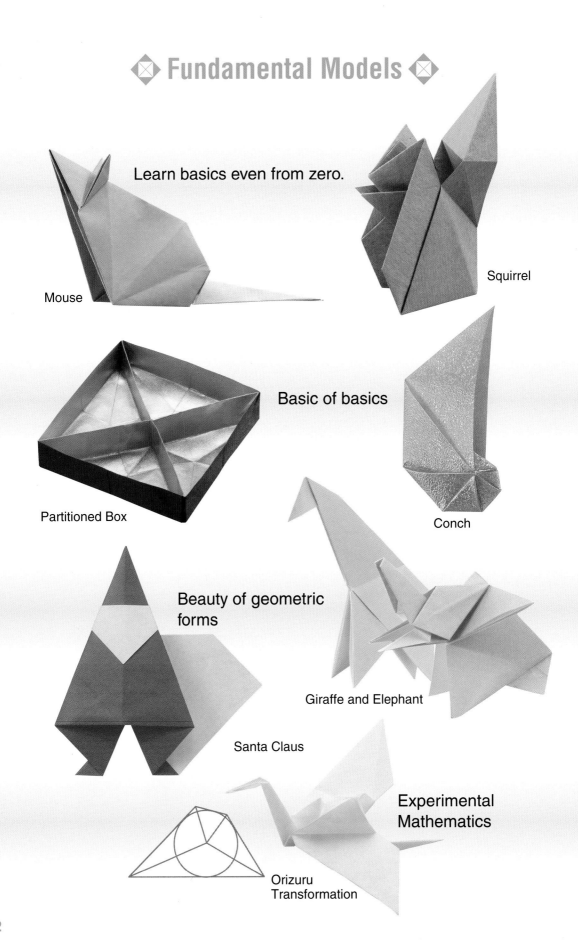

Learn basics even from zero.

Mouse

Squirrel

Basic of basics

Partitioned Box

Conch

Beauty of geometric forms

Santa Claus

Giraffe and Elephant

Experimental Mathematics

Orizuru Transformation

◆ Simple Models ◆

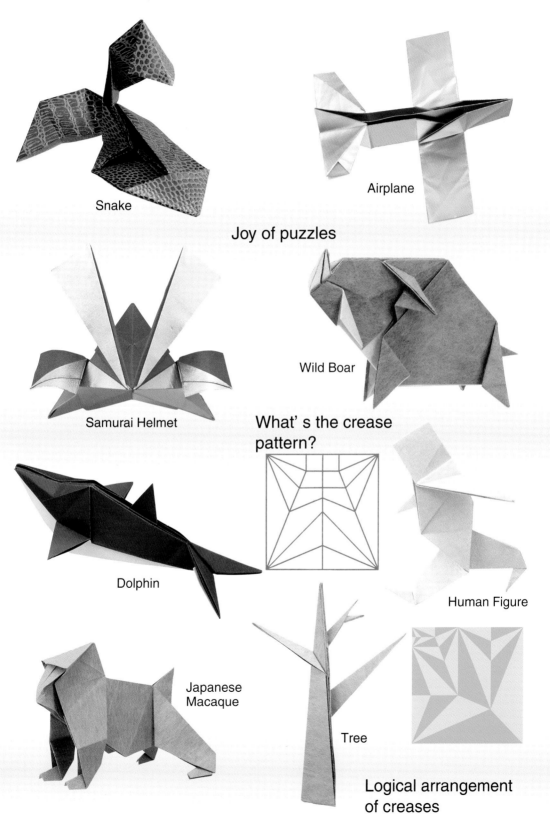

Snake

Airplane

Joy of puzzles

Samurai Helmet

Wild Boar

What's the crease pattern?

Dolphin

Human Figure

Japanese Macaque

Tree

Logical arrangement of creases

◈ Varieties of Origami ◈

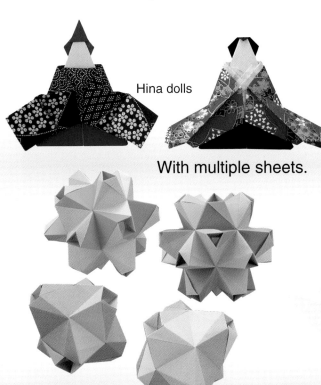

Hina dolls

With multiple sheets.

Tea-bag Reindeer

With any kind of paper.

Fujiyama Module

Connected Cranes, Kotobuki

Even with cuts.

◈ Intermediate Models ◈

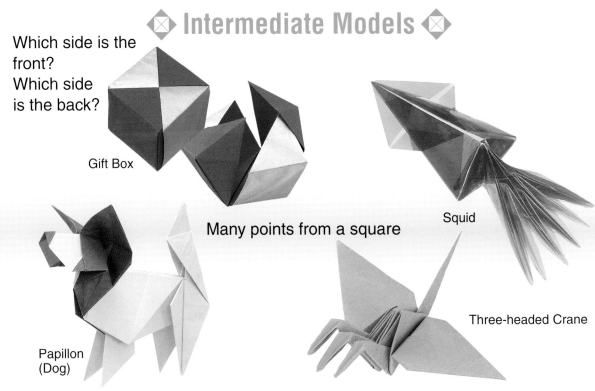

Which side is the front?
Which side is the back?

Gift Box

Many points from a square

Squid

Three-headed Crane

Papillon (Dog)

◈ Intermediate Models ◈

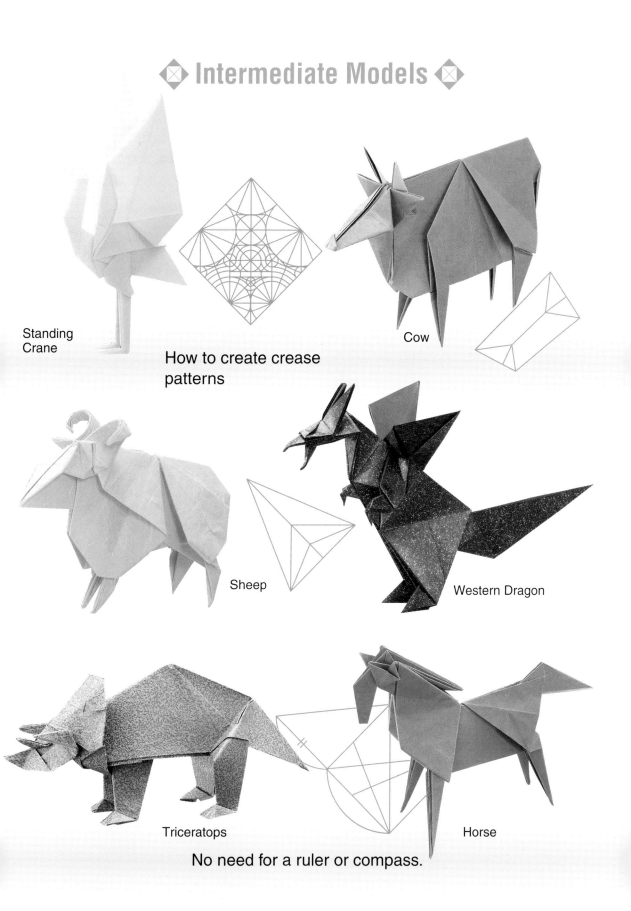

Standing
Crane

How to create crease
patterns

Cow

Sheep

Western Dragon

Triceratops

Horse

No need for a ruler or compass.

5

◈ Intermediate Models ◈

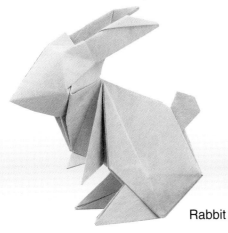

Rabbit

From planes to
solid bodies.

Tiger Mask

Devil Mask

From planes to
curved surfaces.

Penguin

Frog

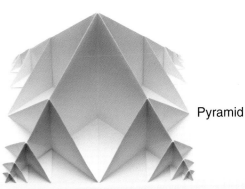

Pyramid

You can fold forever.

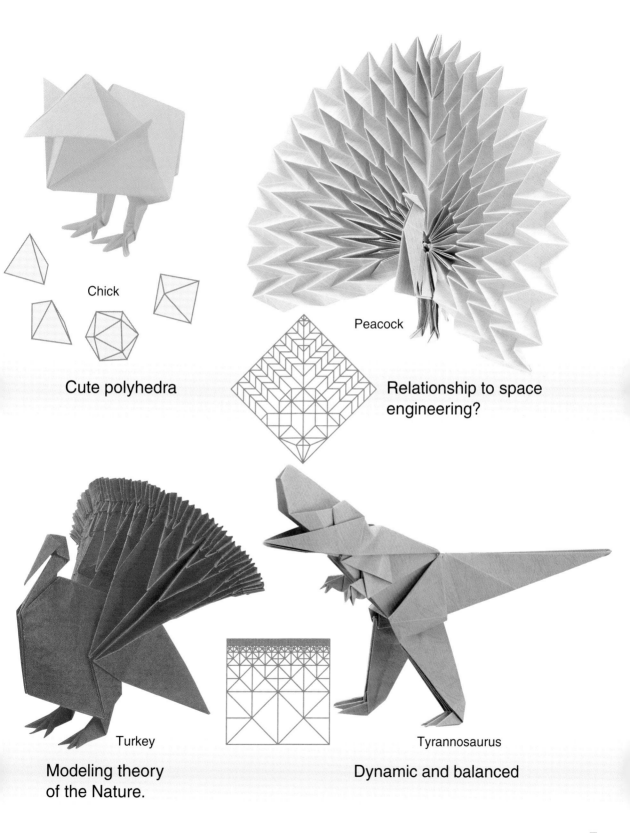

Chick

Cute polyhedra

Peacock

Relationship to space
engineering?

Turkey

Modeling theory
of the Nature.

Tyrannosaurus

Dynamic and balanced

You had been initiated into the secrets when you fold these.

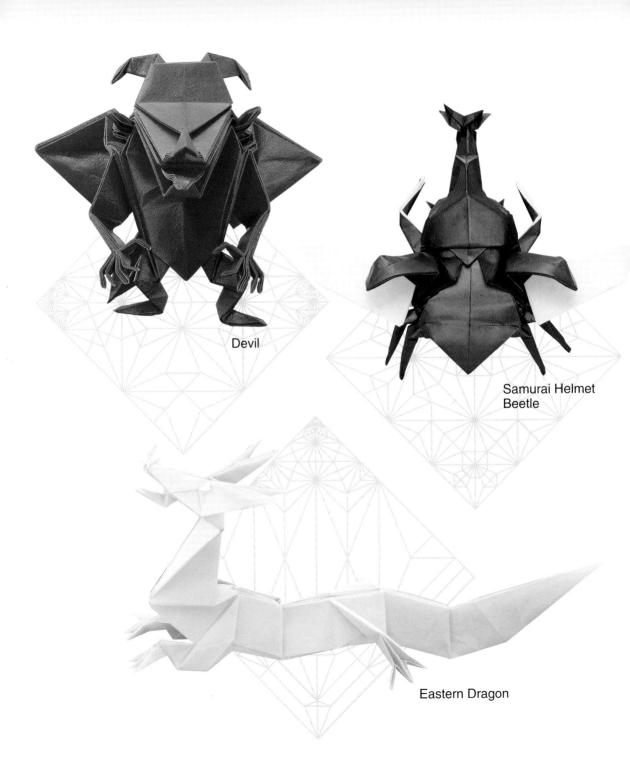

Devil

Samurai Helmet
Beetle

Eastern Dragon

"Origami space has an inner richness that makes our own space look bland."
Barrington J. Bayley, The Exploration of Space

"The most important moral for me is that we sometimes have to make bold to reduce imaginative phenomena to 'geometrized' basic problems."
Pierre Boulez, Le pays fertile: Paul Klee

"My goal was not to make works of art, but to discover the potentiality of shapes through exercise of the brain. I had no brave will such that to shape voices echoing in my heart or to express my soul."
Masakazu Horiuchi on his sculpture

I have written this book with an ambitious aim. I want those who only made some simple models in their childhood to rediscover the joys of origami. At the same time I want those who fold origami as a hobby to spend a meaningful time to develop a better understanding about origami.

That is the reason why this book looks like a rather serious textbook. Each model has its theme, and many are accompanied by some paragraphs about geometry. But it is still an origami book. I hope, above all, while folding the models presented in this book, you will enjoy exercising your brain and fingers.

Although the variety of the models is restricted by the overall composition, this book covers all of the Chinese zodiacs, the rooster being represented by the chick, as well as some seasonal models.

I believe all of the models in this book are origami-like. By the word "origami-like," I mean, conscious of a shape according to geometry, filled with sense of discovery, and designed with paper.

Having said that, I am myself still on the way to understanding the meaning of the word. Maybe what I mean is just something for my taste. I would say this book is an endeavor to examine the notion of "origami-like."

I hope that my view of the word will correspond with your experiences of joy of origami at some point. And that you will find in this book some models that you want to fold repeatedly, some models that you want to teach to others, or some models or sentences from which you find clues to create your own models.

◇ Table of Contents ◇

Intermediate Models 59

Complex Models 107

◈ Introduction ◈

This book consists of five chapters, **Fundamental Models, Simple Models, Varieties of Origami, Intermediate Models, and Complex Models**.

This composition is intended so that even beginners can step up their ability to make complex models by following it in order.

Those who have already mastered the basics, however, should not be bored with the ostensibly easy models in **Simple Models**, as they are full of various ideas. Also, I do not think they are on a low level of design because they are simple. I even like some of them more than the models in **Complex Models**.

The third chapter **Varieties of Origami** is a little interlude. Although this book mainly deals with the mainstream of origami, that is, design with a single sheet of square paper without cuts, the models in this chapter with multi-sheets or cuts demonstrate that origami is more than "one square sheet without cuts."

The most significant characteristic of this book is that each model **has its own theme**, such as "Understand symbols" or "Base". The idea is to enable you to understand various techniques and ways of thinking by folding the actual models.

The themes are explained in **the boxes that are included in the diagrams**.

The explanations contain text to assist you to design your own models. They also contain topics about geometry, which is one of the centerpieces of origami.

As you will see, this book is filled with annotations. I would say this is a **textbook of origami**, teaching through the introduction of my origami models.

You can, of course, **skip the explanations and start to make any models you like without paying attention to the order of models or themes. However, when you stumble upon a step, look up the index to go back to the page where the technique is first illustrated, which will help you to solve the problem**.

Well, I may be getting too serious. I believe you can enjoy this book by just completing the models one by one, as if you are playing a video game.

In Japan, low-priced packages of origami paper are available everywhere, even at many convenience stores. Most of them contain 6" (15 cm) square sheets (same size as this box) of thin paper, white on one side and solid color on the other.

Such paper is suitable for many of the models in this book. But a 6" sheet may be too small to make a complex model. Moreover, you may not be satisfied with the quality of origami paper when you display your own models.

You can purchase origami paper, even in large sheets such as 10" (25 cm) or 12" (30 cm) square, at large art-supply or stationery stores. Though this kind of paper is easy to fold, any other paper can be used in origami. There are so many kinds of paper surrounding you, fliers, wrappers, copy paper, and so on. You can just cut them into squares or other required shapes.

You can find many more kinds of paper at large stores. It is fun to choose among such beautiful sheets. Thick sheets, however, are not suitable for origami unless you use them in huge sizes. Choose paper thinner than 24 lb/ream* (90 g/m^2).

Thin and strong washi (Japanese handmade paper), such as gampi, is also suitable for origami. You can use glue as a finishing touch, or choose crisp paper so that a sheet will hold creases well. Sometimes you need a sheet with a different color on each side. You can use packaged origami paper, or print a solid color with a computer if you do not have adequate paper.

I said "cut them into squares" above, and you may think cutting is "prohibited" in origami. However, even the strictest folders who adhere to the "no cuts" rule do cut paper to obtain squares.

Square sheets are rare, except for paper napkins, medicine wrapping glassine paper, liner notes of vinyl records, or Thai 60 baht notes issued to celebrate King Bhumibol Adulyadej's 60th birthday. Well, vinyl records or Thai commemorative notes themselves are also rare, though. Although they are rare around us, we use square sheets of paper for most of origami. Why square? In addition, why not cut, and how many sheets to use? I will examine these questions later in **Varieties of Origami**.

I recommend suitable paper for each model right after its title. At the end of this book, I have appended information about the types and sizes of paper I used for the models in the pictures at the beginning of the book, which may also be helpful.

* 1 ream is usually 500 sheets.

◈ Symbols and Basic Folds ◈

Before you start to make origami models, you must be familiar with the symbols and terms that have special meanings in origami.

Though there is no rule or code about the symbols, there is a standard set of symbols that is used in many origami books. I adopt that convention, which is shown below. In addition, as I have said in **Introduction**, explanations of symbols and terms are included in the diagrams so that you will be able to learn them by folding each model.

There are many techniques that are not explained in this page, but they are explained along with the diagrams. Refer the index at the end of this book.

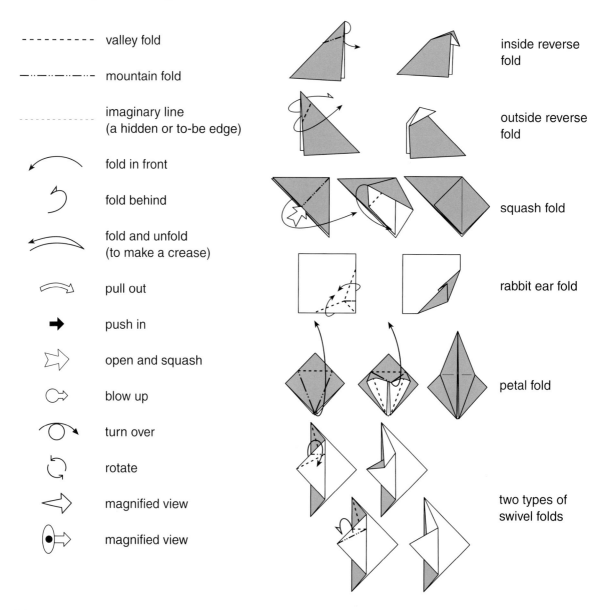

- - - - - - - - - valley fold

—·—··—··—··- mountain fold

- - - - - - - - imaginary line (a hidden or to-be edge)

fold in front

fold behind

fold and unfold (to make a crease)

pull out

push in

open and squash

blow up

turn over

rotate

magnified view

magnified view

inside reverse fold

outside reverse fold

squash fold

rabbit ear fold

petal fold

two types of swivel folds

Mouse

Theme: Understand symbols
Explains basic symbols as well as techniques including inside reverse folds and rabbit ear folds.

Squirrel

Theme: Base
Looks into the base, which is a halfway shape that appears in the course of a sequence. Also explains pleat folds and other techniques.

Partitioned Box

Theme: Bird base
Explains the Bird base, the most important base of all, although in a slightly bizarre way.

Conch

Theme: Trisection; Isosceles right triangle
Shows one of the sequences that trisect precisely a side. Also, explores the shape of isosceles right triangles.

Chapter 1

Fundamental Models

" 'Excellent !' I cried. 'Elementary.' said he."
Arthur Conan Doyle, Memories of Sherlock Holmes

Santa Claus

Theme: Inside-out
Introduces an example of model that uses the different colors of each side of the paper. Also explains swivel folds.

Giraffe

Theme: "Mitate"; Sink fold
An example of model that use "mitate," a form of expression where a simple shape is compared to another. Also explains sink folds.

Elephant

Theme: Blintz fold; Outside reverse fold
Illustrates the blintz fold as one of devices for origami design. Also explains outside reverse folds.

Orizuru Transformation

Theme: Geometry
Examines the geometry of origami by looking into the transformation of origami crane.

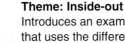

Mouse

Theme: Understand symbols
Fold using 6" (15 cm) origami paper.

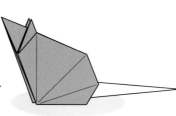

The first model is the *Mouse*, which is the first animal of the Chinese zodiac. Since the theme is to understand symbols, I have included several annoyingly-plentiful notes. Make sure to look through them.

A dashed line indicates a valley fold. A reflected arrow represents **to fold and unfold**, i.e. to make a crease.

A black-headed arrow indicates **to fold**. That means almost all folds except mountain folds are expressed by such arrow.

 It may be easier to fold in the orientation shown on the left. It is often the case that you can fold easier in a different orientation than indicated in diagrams. Also note that a pair of rotating arrows changes orientation of the model, as in step 4.

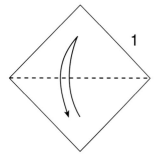

1

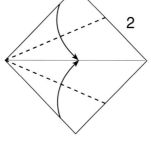

2

 An inflating arrow means **magnified view next**.

3

A pair of black dots (as in steps 3, 4, 9, 10) emphasizes that the points are to meet each other.

When you follow diagrams, always compare the previous step with the next one to identify the changes in shape.

A white circle (as in step 6) emphasizes a landmark of a crease line.

A dot-and-dash line indicates a mountain fold. A white-headed arrow means fold behind. In practice, it is sometimes easier to turn over and valley fold.

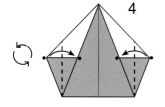

4

5

6

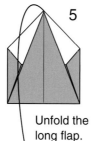

Unfold the long flap.

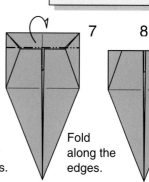

7   8

Tuck the tip under the layers.

Fold along the edges.

Unfold.

9   10   11

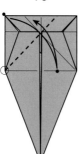

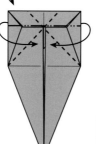

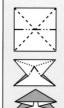

12

In steps 11-12, you fold like a **Water-bomb base**, which is illustrated on the left. The Water-bomb base is a halfway shape of traditional Water-bomb shown on the right.

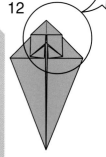

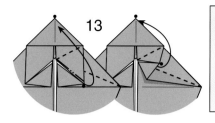

Step 13 is a kind of **rabbit ear fold**, though not a typical one. You make three new creases (two valley folds and one mountain fold) at once to make a triangular flap. Refer to the next model Squirrel for a typical swivel fold.

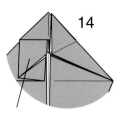

A white thick arrow as in step 15 indicates **to pull out (an inner point etc.)**. In this case, you may have to slightly unfold some creases because some layers are interlocked. This arrow sometimes indicates just to pull.

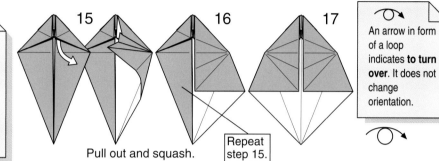

Pull out and squash.

Repeat step 15.

An arrow in form of a loop indicates **to turn over**. It does not change orientation.

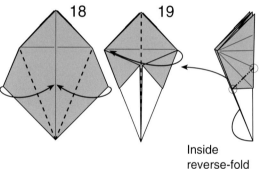

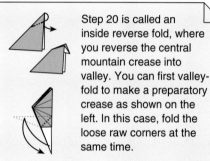

Inside reverse-fold

In progress. Bottom-side view of step 20

Step 20 is called an inside reverse fold, where you reverse the central mountain crease into valley. You can first valley-fold to make a preparatory crease as shown on the left. In this case, fold the loose raw corners at the same time.

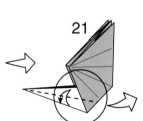

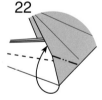

Make a preparatory crease.

Inside reverse-fold

Step 22 may look different from step 20, but it is still an example of inside reverse fold.

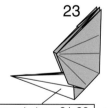

Repeat steps 21-22.

Repeat steps 26-30.

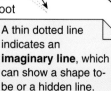

Inside reverse-fold at the root

A thin dotted line indicates an **imaginary line**, which can show a shape to-be or a hidden line.

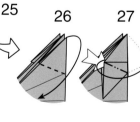

A white arrow as in step 27 indicates **to open a pocket and squash**.

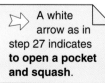

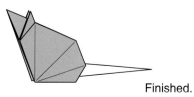

Finished.

Squirrel

Theme: Base

Fold using 6" (15 cm) origami paper.

> Step 5 is called a **Fish base**. And steps 3-4 show a typical **rabbit ear fold**. You can see that a Fish base consists of two rabbit ear folds.

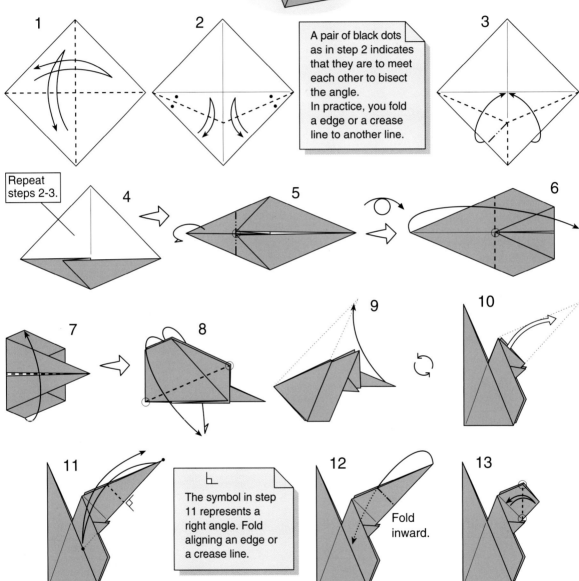

1

2

> A pair of black dots as in step 2 indicates that they are to meet each other to bisect the angle.
> In practice, you fold a edge or a crease line to another line.

3

Repeat steps 2-3.

4

5

6

7

8

9

10

11

> The symbol in step 11 represents a right angle. Fold aligning an edge or a crease line.

12

Fold inward.

13

Tips: How to fold neatly (Part 1)
To fold origami models (at least the models in this book), you should fold accurately and firmly as a general rule. In diagrams, we usually draw layers as though they are not aligned to emphasize overlap of them. But you must fold precisely according to landmarks, which are shown as black dots or white circles, and descriptions. Moreover, unless otherwise stated, it is better to crease sharply, even using your nails, to make a good-looking model.

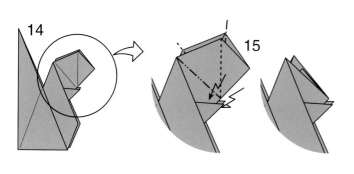

> ⚡➤ A zigzag arrow indicates **to pleat** or **to crimp**. In this case, you make angled pleats symmetrically on both layers to push the layers inward. This is sometimes called an **inside crimp**.

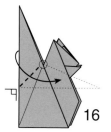

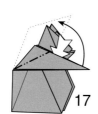

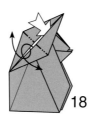

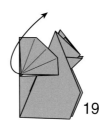

Squash-fold. Squash-fold. Open the tail to make it 3D. Open the body slightly to finish.

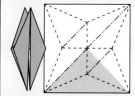

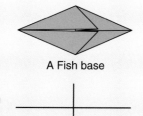

The crease pattern of a Fish base.

A Fish base

The tree structure of the Fish base

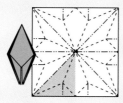

Fish (a.k.a. Carp)

A Bird base and its crease pattern

A Frog base (a.k.a. Iris base) and its crease pattern

The tree structure of the Bird base

The tree structure of the Frog base

Base

The name Fish base comes from traditional *Fish* (also known as *Carp*). This base is characterized by two long flaps and two short ones. In *Squirrel*, I have used two short flaps for the forelegs, one long flap for the tail, and the other for the body, and omitted the hind legs. Such flap-based design is one of the basic methods of origami design.

Bases have played an important role as starting point for design of various models. For example, the *Squirrel* starts from a Fish base. However, in recent years of creative origami, similar to inside reverse folds, it may be more accurate to regard bases as just another folding technique. I have already explained a step in *Mouse* as "fold like a Water-bomb base", which suggests that a base is a sort of fold technique.

There are about 10 important types of bases, which are described in this page and other parts of this book. The most important of all is the Bird base, which is in the same class as the Fish base, as well as the Frog base (also known as the Iris base).

You will figure out the reason why I say they are in the same class if you look at the crease patterns, or the creases left on unfolded sheets, of the bases.

Look at the crease patterns carefully. If we cut a Fish base in half along its diagonal line, we have a unit. A Bird base consists of four units, and a Frog base eight. One can also say a Frog base is composed of four Fish bases.

Partitioned Box

Theme: Bird base

Fold using 6" (15 cm) origami paper.

I made use of the symmetry of the Bird base to design this model. Pay attention to the orientation in the steps 13, 14, and 23. It will be also interesting to start with colored side up.

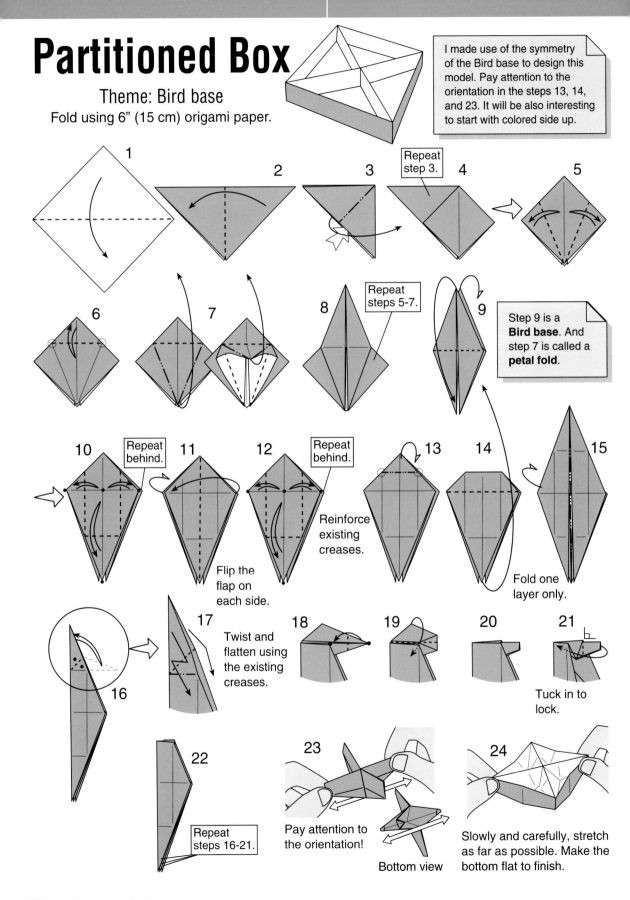

1

2

3

Repeat step 3.

4

5

6

7

8

Repeat steps 5-7.

9

Step 9 is a **Bird base**. And step 7 is called a **petal fold**.

10

Repeat behind.

11

12

Repeat behind.

13

14

15

Reinforce existing creases.

Flip the flap on each side.

Fold one layer only.

16

17

Twist and flatten using the existing creases.

18

19

20

21

Tuck in to lock.

22

Repeat steps 16-21.

23

Pay attention to the orientation!

Bottom view

24

Slowly and carefully, stretch as far as possible. Make the bottom flat to finish.

Conch

Theme: Trisection; Isosceles right triangle
Fold using 6" (15 cm) origami paper.

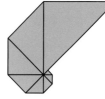

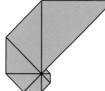

Trisection
The first two steps 1-2 indicates the point that trisects the side of a square precisely, which is indicated as A. Kazuo Haga formulated this method of trisection, hence it is called Haga theorem.

The right diagram shows the key to prove the theorem. The ratio of three sides on each gray triangle is 3 : 4 : 5.

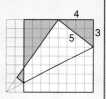

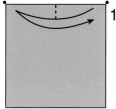
1
Pinch.

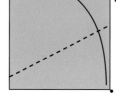
2

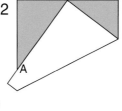
3

A

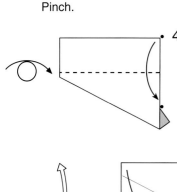
4

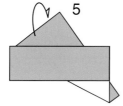
5

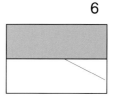
6

7

8

9

10

11

12

13

14

15

16

17

Tuck in.

Finished.

Isosceles right triangle

In *Squirrel*, we have seen that the Fish, Bird, and Frog bases is made up in a systematic series. That is because the bases are composed of same basic shapes, each of which is an isosceles right triangle, or a triangle that is a half of a square. When you divide an isosceles right triangle in two equal parts, each will be similar in proportion to the original figure. Besides the triangles, only parallelograms with ratio 1 : √2 share this property. *Conch* starts with a trisection, and makes use of the property that when divided into half, it generates two parts, each similar in proportion to the original shape. The picture above also exploit this property, and it graphically represents an equation 1/2 + 1/4 + 1/8 + ... = 1.

Santa Claus

Theme: Inside-out
Fold using 6" (15 cm) origami paper.

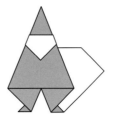

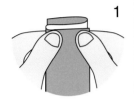

1

You can trisect a side by estimation as in the step 1. This is the best way if you get used to, as you will avoid the diagonal crease line.

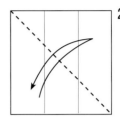

2

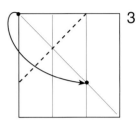

3

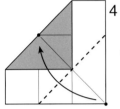

4

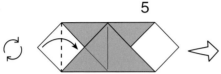

5

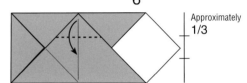

6

Approximately 1/3

7

Fold the edge to the center line.

The two pairs of black dots in step 7 indicate they are to meet each other, which means you fold the edge to the crease line.

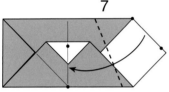

8

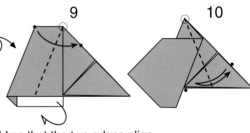

9

10

Fold so that the two edges align, while flipping out the bottom layer.

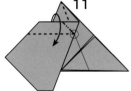

11

Swivel-fold

A Swivel fold is illustrated on the left. It is usually used to make an acute point.

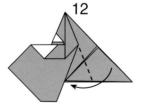

12

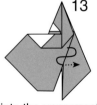

13

Tuck into the uppermost pocket to lock.

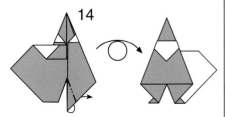

14

Inside reverse-fold   Finished.

Inside-out

This model has both colored and white parts, as Mouse has a white tail. Such a technique of using different colors of each side of paper is called inside-out. Though the technique itself is not new, its name has spread out because of "Origami Inside-Out" by John Montroll, which contains only inside-out models. Note that "inside out" also means thoroughly. On the other hand, the outside surface of a Bird base is covered by only one side of paper, and the inside surface by only the other side. Such property is called one-sidedness, as coined by Kodi Husimi. It also becomes an interesting condition from a geometrical point of view.

Giraffe

Theme: "Mitate"; Sink fold
Fold using 6" (15 cm) origami paper.

"Mitate"
"Mitate" is a Japanese word that means a form of expression where a simple shape is compared to another. In the case of this model, I saw a giraffe in step 9. I think the origin of origami was a game with simple shapes and imagining what it resembled like ("mitate"). Seiji Nishikawa introduced this word into origami.

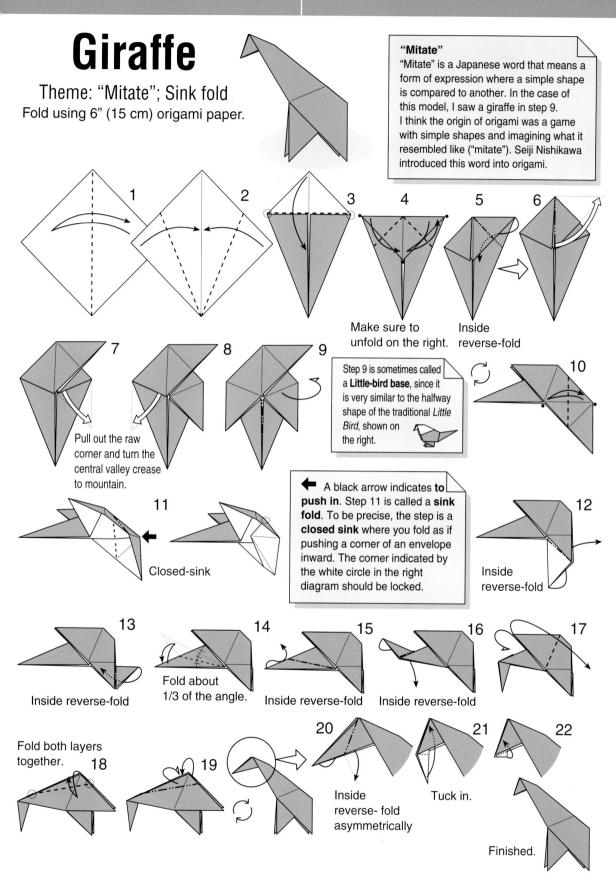

1

2

3

4

5

6

Make sure to unfold on the right.

Inside reverse-fold

7

8

9

Pull out the raw corner and turn the central valley crease to mountain.

Step 9 is sometimes called a **Little-bird base**, since it is very similar to the halfway shape of the traditional *Little Bird*, shown on the right.

10

A black arrow indicates **to push in**. Step 11 is called a **sink fold**. To be precise, the step is a **closed sink** where you fold as if pushing a corner of an envelope inward. The corner indicated by the white circle in the right diagram should be locked.

11

Closed-sink

12

Inside reverse-fold

13

Inside reverse-fold

14

Fold about 1/3 of the angle.

15

Inside reverse-fold

16

Inside reverse-fold

17

Fold both layers together.

18

19

20

Inside reverse- fold asymmetrically

21

Tuck in.

22

Finished.

Elephant

Theme: Blintz fold; Outside reverse fold

Fold using 6" (15 cm) origami paper.

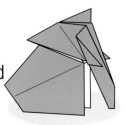

Step 2 is called a blintz fold. Since it doubles the layers of the square, this fold is often used to enhance existing bases or models.

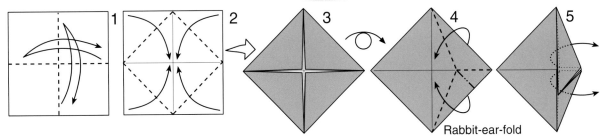

1　　2　　3　　4　　5

Rabbit-ear-fold

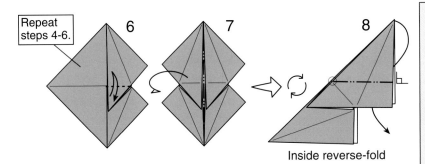

Repeat steps 4-6.

6　　7　　8

Inside reverse-fold

Tips: How to fold neatly (Part 2)
Make sure that all the creases intersect each other precisely at one point. For example, make a nice corner at the white circle in step 8 by folding as far as possible, pulling down as far as the reverse-folded point.
A tiny gap will be amplified in course of the sequence.

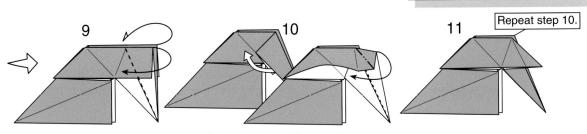

9　　10　　11

Repeat step 10.

Pull out and rabbit-ear-fold.

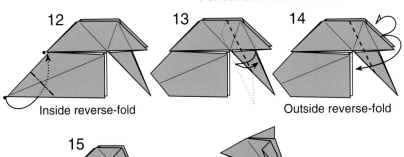

12　　13　　14

Inside reverse-fold　　Outside reverse-fold

The left diagram illustrate an outside reverse fold, where you reverse the central valley crease into mountain. You can first valley-fold to make a preparatory crease, as you have done in the step 13. Also, you will have to slightly open the entire model in order to make this fold.

15

Open the ears to finish.

Here is a slightly modified variation.

Start from step 11.

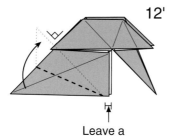

12'

Leave a small gap.

There is no definite landmark for the step 12'. Such fold is called **judgment fold**. Though judgment is not so important with this model, a small difference sometimes results in a very different finish.

13'
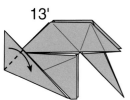

14'
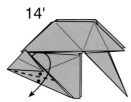

15'
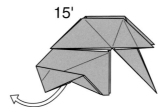

Unfold back to step 12'.

16'
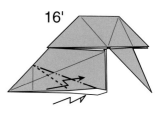

Inside crimp

17'
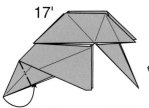

Inside reverse-fold

18'
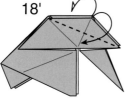

19'
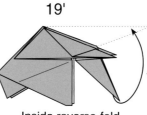

Inside reverse-fold

20'
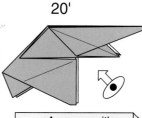

An arrow with an eye represents the viewpoint of the next diagram.

21'
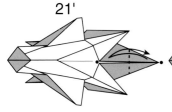

22'
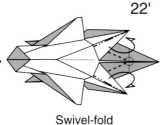

Swivel-fold

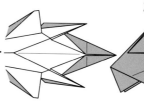

23'
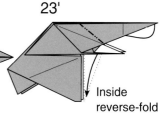

Inside reverse-fold

24'
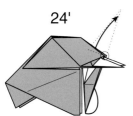

Inside reverse-fold

25'
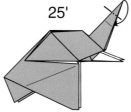

Fold the tip of the trunk inward. Open the ears.

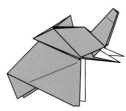

Finished.

Orizuru Transformation

Theme: Geometry
Fold using 6" (15 cm) origami paper.

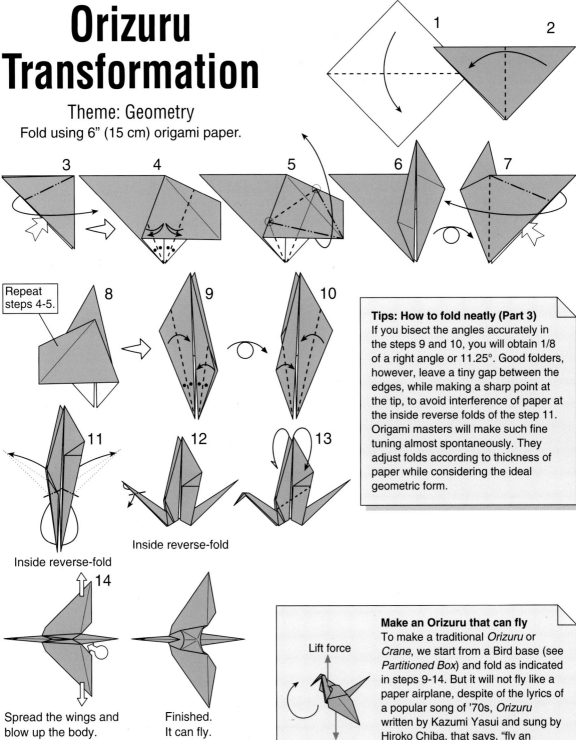

Repeat
steps 4-5.

Tips: How to fold neatly (Part 3)
If you bisect the angles accurately in the steps 9 and 10, you will obtain 1/8 of a right angle or 11.25°. Good folders, however, leave a tiny gap between the edges, while making a sharp point at the tip, to avoid interference of paper at the inside reverse folds of the step 11. Origami masters will make such fine tuning almost spontaneously. They adjust folds according to thickness of paper while considering the ideal geometric form.

Inside reverse-fold

Inside reverse-fold

Spread the wings and blow up the body.

Finished. It can fly.

An arrow with a circle as in step 14 indicates to blow up. Although you do not have to blow in this case, blowing into an orizuru has some magical meaning, according to one theory.

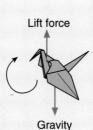

Lift force

Gravity

Make an Orizuru that can fly
To make a traditional *Orizuru* or *Crane*, we start from a Bird base (see *Partitioned Box*) and fold as indicated in steps 9-14. But it will not fly like a paper airplane, despite of the lyrics of a popular song of '70s, *Orizuru* written by Kazumi Yasui and sung by Hiroko Chiba, that says, "fly an orizuru." It will turn upward because its center of gravity is behind the center of lift force. To be able to fly, an orizuru must have a heavier head, or sweepback wings as this model has. This transformed orizuru can fly.

Geometry of Orizuru Transformation

In this section, I will explain the geometry of *Orizuru Transformation* referring to studies by Kodi Husimi, Jacques Justin, Toshiyuki Meguro, Toshikazu Kawasaki, and others.

You have squash-folded asymmetrically in the step 3 of this model, whereas you fold to make a square in a regular orizuru. You can squash-fold at an arbitrary angle, not only the angle specified.
Moreover, you can fold in a different angle on each side, as shown on the left.

This transformation does not prevent to complete an orizuru because the transformed Bird base has the same property as the regular one. Because the base has no loose raw edge, all of the outside surface of the base is covered by one side of paper, and all of the inside covered by the other side.
This property is called one-sidedness, as coined by Kodi Husimi.
Also important is that the base of a wing is a single straight line.
The crease pattern on the right will not make a transformed orizuru because the base of a wing will be split in two lines.

Then, what is the basic feature of the Bird base?

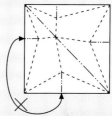

They will not match.

As we have seen in **Bases** *(see Squirrel)*, a Bird base is composed of four rabbit-ear-folded isosceles right triangles, as shown on the right.

A rabbit ear fold is possible because three bisectors of angles on a triangle intersect each other at one point. The point is the **inner center**, or the center of the inscribed circle, of the triangle.

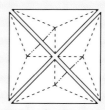

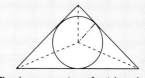

The inner center of a triangle

A rabbit ear fold

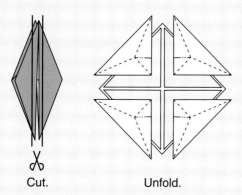

Cut. Unfold.

Divide a regular Bird base into its basic units.

All of three edges of a triangle will be aligned with a rabbit ear fold. A Bird base has four rabbit ear folds, and all of their edges also align.
Toshiyuki Meguro has demonstrated this alignment clearly in an interesting way.

Imagine you cut a Bird base along its "center line" that has some thickness.
In practice, you are going to cut twice, as shown on the right, instead of cutting once with thick scissors.

When you unfold the divided parts, you will find that the square is divided into four rabbit ear folds.
Remember the remaining frame, which consists of four edges and two diagonals of the square, was a single line in the Bird base.

Whereas a regular Bird base consists of triangles, each of which are rabbit-ear- folded, the base of *Orizuru Transformation* consists of kite-shaped quadrangles. When I realized that each unit can be a combination of two arbitrary triangles, I still thought the units are basically triangles and called the transformation of orizuru "Tri-inner-center theorem." But cutting a transformed Bird base along its center line reveals its essence clearly.

As you can see on the right, a base will be divided into quadrangles. And it is no surprise.

Even when you rabbit-ear-fold a triangle, you need one extra crease that is perpendicular to a side, besides three bisectors, to fold it flat. We can see the intersection of the crease and the side (the foot of the perpendicular) as fourth corner of a quadrangle, a corner with a 180° angle. Then, the Bird base consists of quadrangles, not triangles. Not all quadrangles, however, can be a unit. Four creases on a quadrangle will align the sides only if the quadrangle has an inscribed circle. If not, we need more than four creases to fold so that the sides align.

In fact, we have rabbit-ear-folded a quadrangle at the step 13 of Mouse, the first model of this book. By the way, a concave quadrangle can have an inscribed circle if the circle is tangent to two sides and two extended lines of the other sides.

Though I did not explain here in detail, the original shape of paper can be any quadrangle, not only a square, as long as it has an inscribed circle. Toshikazu Kawasaki has proved that any quadrangle that has an inscribed circle can be divided into four quadrangles, each of which has also an inscribed circle, which can be folded to make an orizuru.

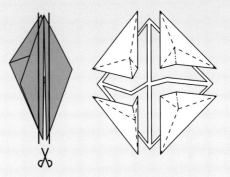

Divide a transformed Bird base into units.

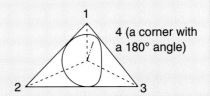

In fact, a unit has four corners, hence it is a quadrangle.

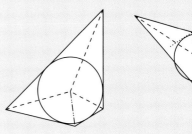

A quadrangle can be rabbit-ear- folded if it has an inscribed circle.

I have explained, in some detail, the transformation of orizuru that exemplifies the close relationship between origami and geometry. *Orizuru Transformation* is "fundamental" as an origami model, but its implication is by no means "fundamental."

In other words, even a simple model conceals geometry in it. Making an origami model is a mathematical experience, even if you do not realize it.

One of the keywords here is one-sidedness. That means, when you make a Bird base, you are dividing the two sides of paper into the inside and the outside.

An avant-garde artist Genpei Akasegawa once created a can labeled inside and titled it *Canned Universe*. With this art-work, he inverted the inside and the outside, wrapping up the whole universe, except the volume of the can, "in" the can.

You can do the same thing with orizuru. If you make a Bird base starting with colored side up, you make a Bird base that contain the whole universe inside.

Snake

Theme: Box pleating
An example of model that is based on box-pleating or square-grid creases. This model is "longer" than the diagonal of the original square.

Airplane

Theme: Repeat on the other side
Gives you some hints about "repeat on the other side," which is sometimes difficult to fold when following diagrams.

Samurai Helmet

Theme: Half-open
Looks into a half-open technique, which is one of the techniques to make a three-dimensional model.

Wild Boar

Theme: 22.5° and $\sqrt{2}$
Shows significance of the 22.5° angle, which is a quarter of the right angle, and the close relation to the $\sqrt{2}$ length.

Chapter 2

Simple Models

Guest speaker: Now, that was my very simple address...
Audience: (There is nothing simple about this address.)

Dolphin

Theme: Shaping
Looks into shaping, which is another technique to make a three-dimensional model.

Human Figure

Theme: Crease pattern
Looks into the crease pattern, which is the interesting pattern of creases observed when unfolding completely the paper.

Japanese Macaque

Theme: Crease pattern fold
Explains a fairly complex sink fold that can be folded easily with the understanding of the crease pattern.

Tree

Theme: Theorem
Shows a couple of geometric theorems about flat-foldable crease patterns.

Snake

Theme: Box pleating
Fold using 6" (15 cm) origami paper.

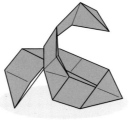

This snake is "longer" than the diagonal of the square. I got the basic idea from another origami snake designed by Masao Okamura.

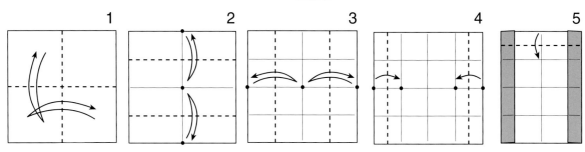

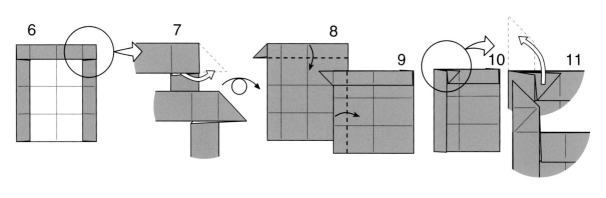

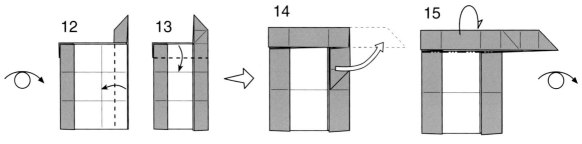

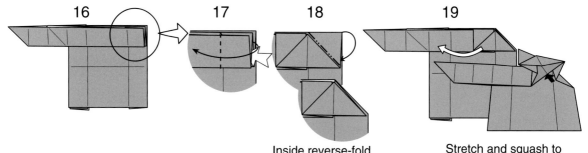

Inside reverse-fold

Stretch and squash to make a trapezoid.

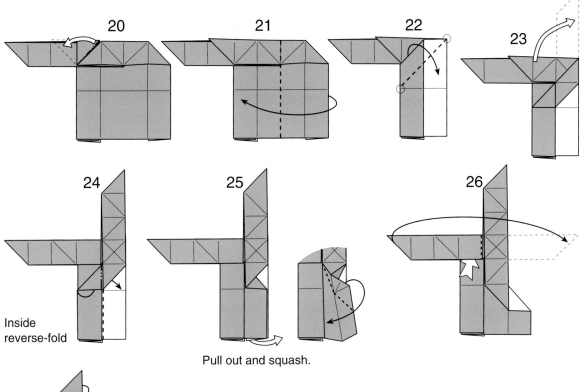

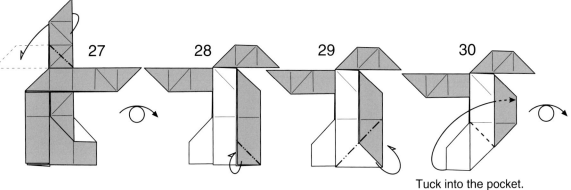

24
Inside
reverse-fold

25
Pull out and squash.

26

27 28 29 30

Tuck into the pocket.

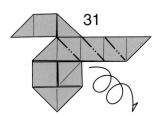

31
Fold over and over.

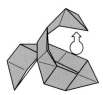

Stand up the neck and
pop up the head to
finish.

Box Pleating
In origami, **box pleating** are folds based on a square grid.
We use box pleating to design origami models mainly for one or both of the
following purposes.
1. To isolate a point using pleats.
2. To obtain an interesting design using shades of pleats.

The use in Snake is a typical example of the former.
An example of the latter is that of Peacock in **Complex Models**. Among the
techniques (or structures) of controlling lengths of points with box pleat, the
most basic fold is a squash fold to make a trapezoid, as in steps 19- 20.
While this model is based on the 8 x 8 grid, much more complex design can
be achieved with the 16 x 16 or finer grid.

Airplane

Theme: Repeat on the other side
Fold using 6" (15 cm) origami paper.

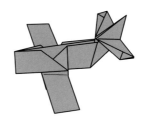

In step 17, you are required to repeat the previous ten steps. You may get stuck with such a long "repeat on the other side" sequence in the diagram because:

1. the sequence is not exactly the same but becomes a mirrored image, and
2. one side is already folded but the other is not, so they are not exactly mirrored images.

One can say the repeating sequence should be shown explicitly or in a smarter way in a diagram. But I challenge you to repeat a long sequence here. Some models in this book have even longer repeating sequences. Such diagrams may be unfriendly, but, in my opinion, folding based on mirrored images is a good exercise for your brain. However, I suggest two ways to manage a "repeat on the other side" sequence.

Two ways to manage a "repeat on the other side" sequence

1. Fold both sides at each step.
For example, inside reverse-fold on both sides at step 8. It is, however, sometimes impossible.
Note that I added the repeat sign used in the music notation (starts with ‖: and ends with :‖) for long repeating steps in this book to show you where to start and where to stop.

2. Fold and unfold on one side, then fold the other.
For example, fold through step 17, unfold back to step 7, and fold on the other side. You will fold twice on one side, once as preparation for the more difficult side, where you must fold the mirrored image.
It will be much easier to fold the second time because you already have all the creases.

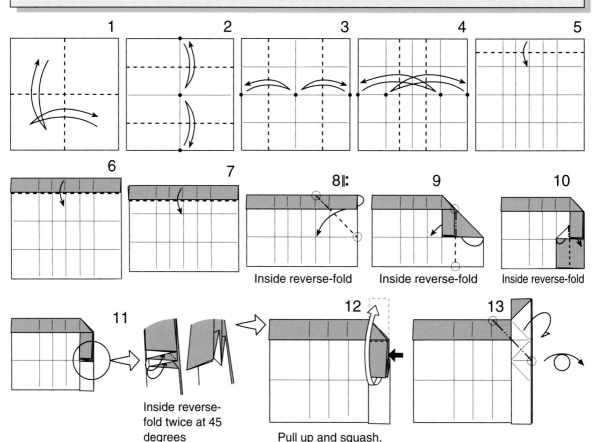

Inside reverse-fold

Inside reverse-fold

Inside reverse-fold

Inside reverse-fold twice at 45 degrees

Pull up and squash.

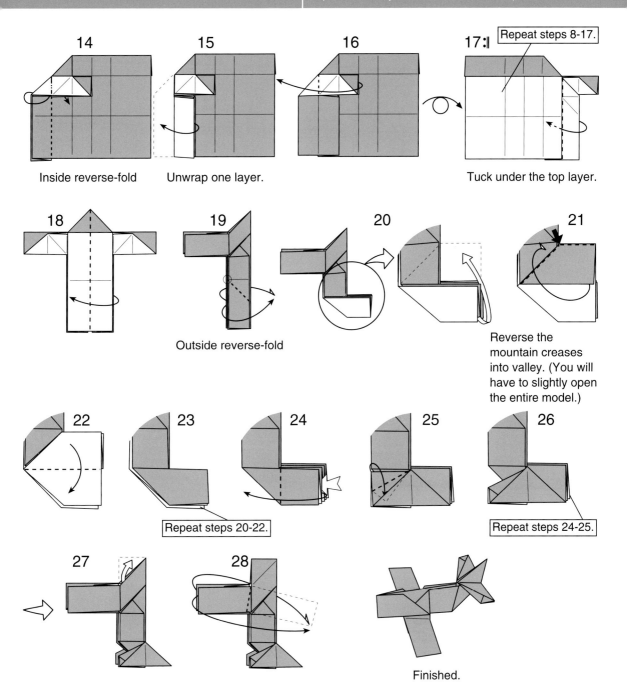

14 Inside reverse-fold

15 Unwrap one layer.

16

17: Repeat steps 8-17. Tuck under the top layer.

18

19 Outside reverse-fold

20

21 Reverse the mountain creases into valley. (You will have to slightly open the entire model.)

22

23 Repeat steps 20-22.

24

25

26 Repeat steps 24-25.

27

28

Finished.

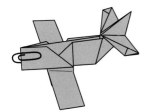

When folded using a sheet of 6" (15 cm) regular origami paper, this model will fly with a paper clip on the nose, although without great flight performance.

There are some origami models that you can play with, such as models that move (either passively by your action or actively with force of unfolding creases) or make sounds. This book does not present such models, but it contains a couple of model that can fly. They are typical examples of action origami.

Samurai Helmet

Theme: Half-open

Fold using 6" (15 cm) origami paper.

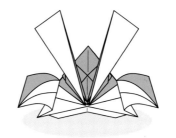

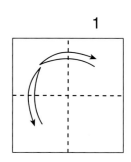
1

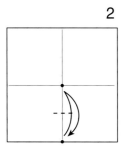
2

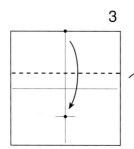
3

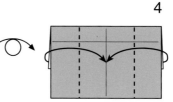
4

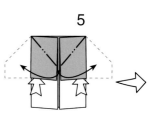
5

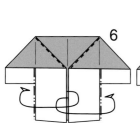
6

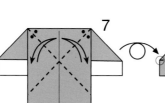
7

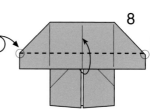
8

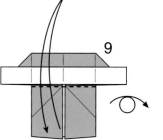
9

Reverse the mountain creases into valley and valley into mountain.

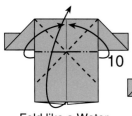
10

Fold like a Water-bomb base using existing creases.

11

Open,

and squash.

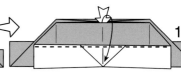
12

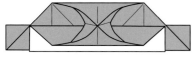

In progress.

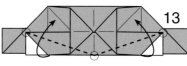
13

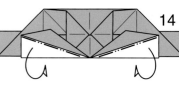
14

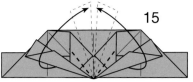

15

16

Fold and unfold the top layer only (the model will not lie flat).

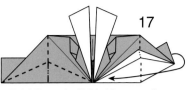

17

Fold like a half Bird-base using the creases made in step 16.

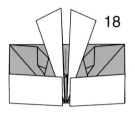

18

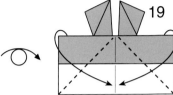

19

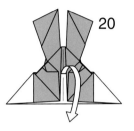

20

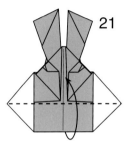

21

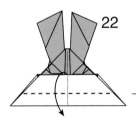

22

about 3
about 2

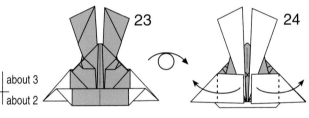

23

24

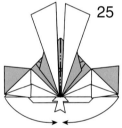

25

Open the model and squash to the side.

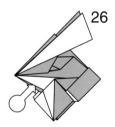

26

Open to make the model 3D.

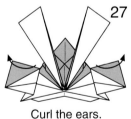

27

Curl the ears.

Half-open

This Samurai Helmet is three-dimensional model, and basically a quadrangle pyramid without a bottom. Of course, helmets do not have a bottom.
Such technique of making 3D models can be called **half-open**.
Kunihiko Kasahara makes use of this technique in the most pure form and calls it **half-open folding**. My Tridacna on the left, folded from a 3 : 2 rectangle, is another example of model using half-open folding.

Tridacna

Finished. The model should stand on the four points.

Wild Boar

Theme: 22.5° and √2
Fold using 6" (15 cm) origami paper.

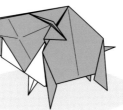

One of the basic angles in origami is 22.5°, which is a quarter of the right angle. This model is based on this angle, as all the creases intersect each other at an angle of 22.5° or its multiples.

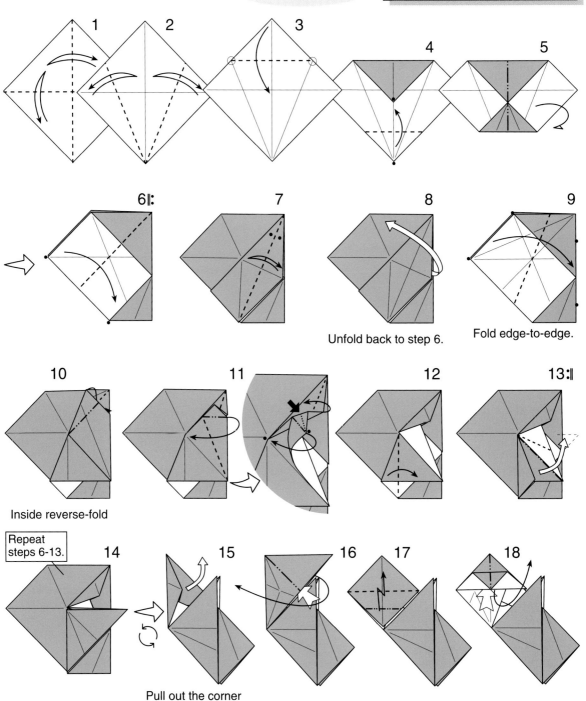

7 Unfold back to step 6.

9 Fold edge-to-edge.

10 Inside reverse-fold

Repeat steps 6-13.

15 Pull out the corner carefully, paying attention not to tear the paper.

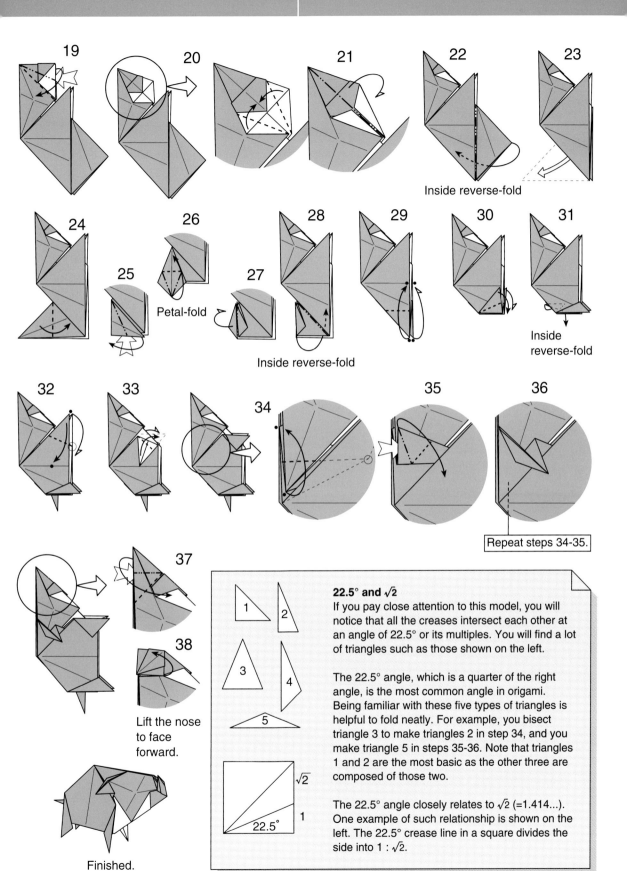

19

20

21

22

23

Inside reverse-fold

24

25

26

Petal-fold

27

Inside reverse-fold

28

29

30

31

Inside reverse-fold

32

33

34

35

36

Repeat steps 34-35.

37

38

Lift the nose to face forward.

Finished.

22.5° and √2

If you pay close attention to this model, you will notice that all the creases intersect each other at an angle of 22.5° or its multiples. You will find a lot of triangles such as those shown on the left.

The 22.5° angle, which is a quarter of the right angle, is the most common angle in origami. Being familiar with these five types of triangles is helpful to fold neatly. For example, you bisect triangle 3 to make triangles 2 in step 34, and you make triangle 5 in steps 35-36. Note that triangles 1 and 2 are the most basic as the other three are composed of those two.

The 22.5° angle closely relates to √2 (=1.414...). One example of such relationship is shown on the left. The 22.5° crease line in a square divides the side into 1 : √2.

Dolphin

Theme: Shaping

Fold using 6" (15 cm) origami paper.

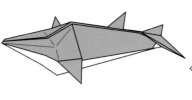

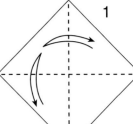

1

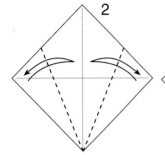

2

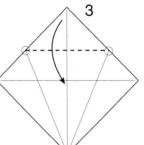

3

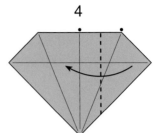

4

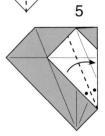

5

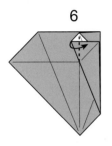

6

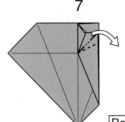

7

8

Repeat steps 4-7.

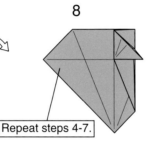

9

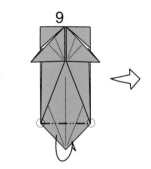

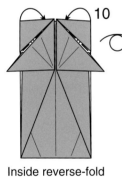

10

Inside reverse-fold

11

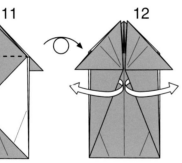

12

Open the model partially.

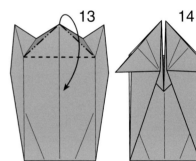

13

14

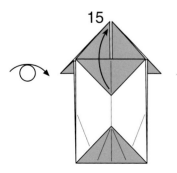

15

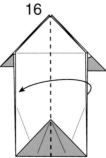

16

17

Inside reverse-fold

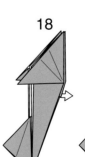

18

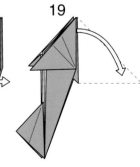

19

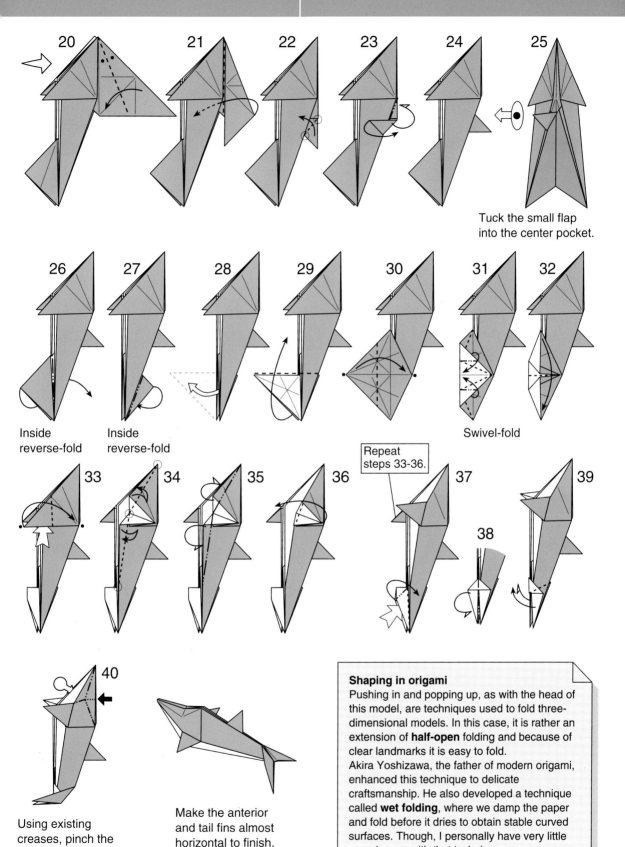

Tuck the small flap into the center pocket.

Inside reverse-fold

Inside reverse-fold

Swivel-fold

Repeat steps 33-36.

Shaping in origami

Pushing in and popping up, as with the head of this model, are techniques used to fold three-dimensional models. In this case, it is rather an extension of **half-open** folding and because of clear landmarks it is easy to fold.

Akira Yoshizawa, the father of modern origami, enhanced this technique to delicate craftsmanship. He also developed a technique called **wet folding**, where we damp the paper and fold before it dries to obtain stable curved surfaces. Though, I personally have very little experiences with that technique.

Using existing creases, pinch the head to make it 3D.

Make the anterior and tail fins almost horizontal to finish.

Human Figure

Theme: Crease pattern
Fold using 6" (15 cm) origami paper.

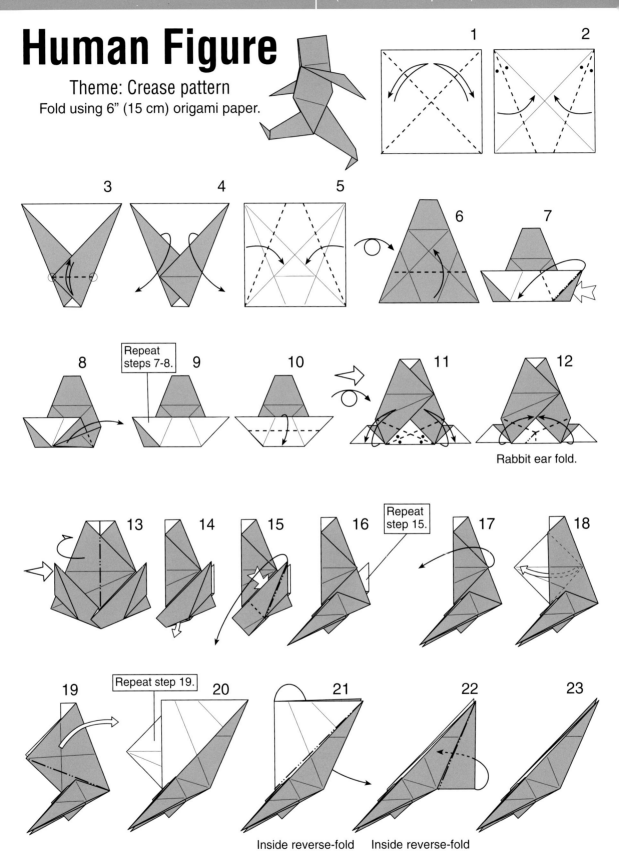

1

2

3

4

5

6

7

8

Repeat steps 7-8.

9

10

11

12

Rabbit ear fold.

13

14

15

Repeat step 15.

16

17

18

19

Repeat step 19.

20

21

22

23

Inside reverse-fold   Inside reverse-fold

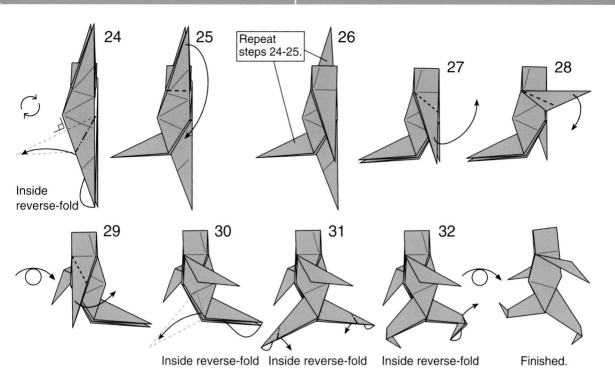

24 **25** Repeat steps 24-25. **26** **27** **28**

Inside reverse-fold

29 **30** **31** **32**

Inside reverse-fold   Inside reverse-fold   Inside reverse-fold   Finished.

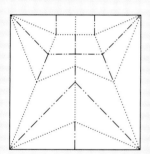

Crease pattern
If you stop folding at step 23 and unfold completely, you will see on the white side of the paper the creases as shown on the left. Such creases, as well as those shown in the **Base** section, is called **crease pattern**.

Although I designed this model a long ago, I came up with this rather tricky sequence through step 23 only when I started writing this book. Noboru Miyajima once created diagrams of this model, but his sequence was far different from mine. My old sequence was also different. I basically pre-creased everything, and collapsed in one step.

When I taught this model, I sometimes distributed a sheet on which the crease pattern was printed and told to collapse according to the lines.

You must be an expert to fold a complex model just from its crease pattern. Moreover, when you fold from the crease pattern, you cannot enjoy the sequence as a story composed by the designer. But this model is an excellent puzzle, when you are supposed to fold the model only from its crease pattern.

In other words, a crease pattern can document a model, in a different way from what can be done using the diagrams.

In addition, as explained later in the book, one can examine the construction of the model using the crease pattern before actually folding it. Such a crease pattern usually does not contain detailed creases.

The pattern for this model has especially few creases. That means, you can pose this human figure as you like. Please find your favorite pose. My favorite is the sitting-on-the-knees pose, as shown on the right. To fold it, mountain-fold the arms in the other direction than in step 28 so that the hands will rest on the knees, and inside reverse-fold the legs twice. For the first inside-reverse fold deeper than in step 24.

Japanese Macaque

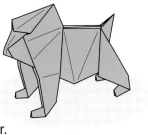

Theme: Crease pattern fold

Fold using 6" (15 cm) origami paper.

1

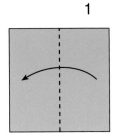

2

3

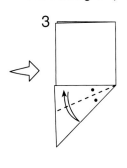

4

Unfold.

5

Inside
reverse-fold

6

7

8

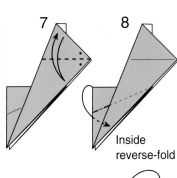

Inside
reverse-fold

9

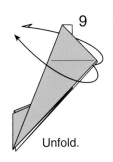

Unfold.

10

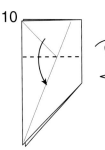

11

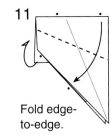

Fold edge-
to-edge.

12

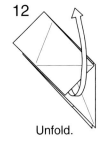

Unfold.

13

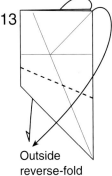

Outside
reverse-fold

14

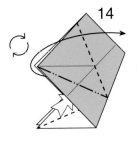

15

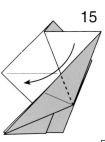

16

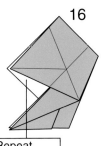

Repeat
steps 14-15.

17

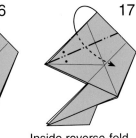

Inside reverse-fold
(Tuck the tip into
any pocket.)

18

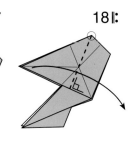

19

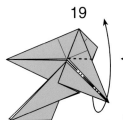

20

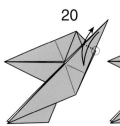

21

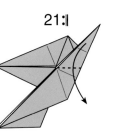

Repeat
steps 18-21.

22

23

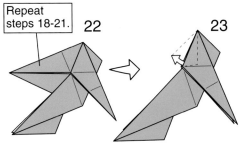

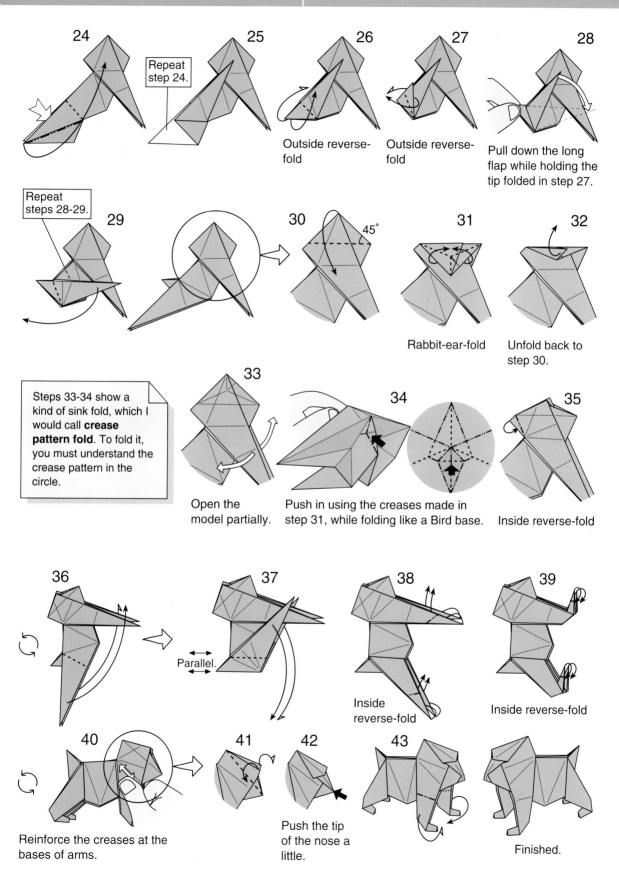

24

25 Repeat step 24.

26 Outside reverse-fold

27 Outside reverse-fold

28 Pull down the long flap while holding the tip folded in step 27.

Repeat steps 28-29.

29

30 45°

31 Rabbit-ear-fold

32 Unfold back to step 30.

Steps 33-34 show a kind of sink fold, which I would call **crease pattern fold**. To fold it, you must understand the crease pattern in the circle.

33 Open the model partially.

34 Push in using the creases made in step 31, while folding like a Bird base.

35 Inside reverse-fold

36

37 Parallel.

38 Inside reverse-fold

39 Inside reverse-fold

40 Reinforce the creases at the bases of arms.

41

42 Push the tip of the nose a little.

43 Finished.

Tree

Theme: Theorem

Fold using 6" (15 cm) origami paper.

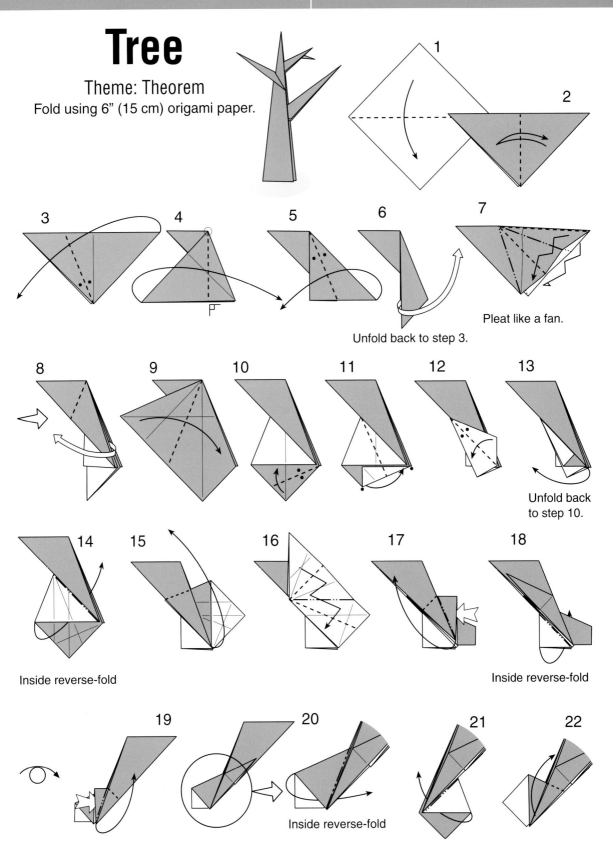

1

2

3

4

5

6

Unfold back to step 3.

7

Pleat like a fan.

8

9

10

11

12

13

Unfold back to step 10.

14

Inside reverse-fold

15

16

17

18

Inside reverse-fold

19

20

Inside reverse-fold

21

22

Inside reverse-fold

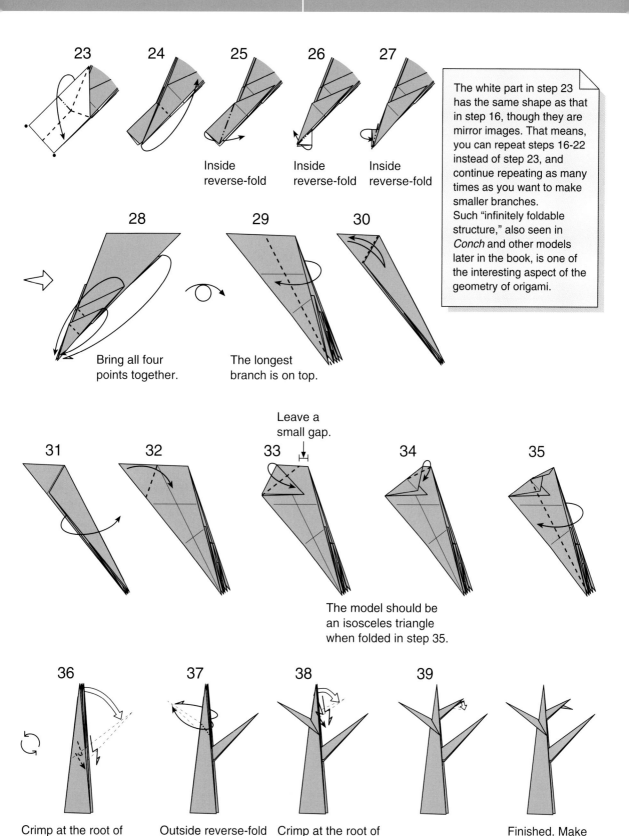

23 **24** **25** **26** **27**

Inside
reverse-fold

Inside
reverse-fold

Inside
reverse-fold

> The white part in step 23
> has the same shape as that
> in step 16, though they are
> mirror images. That means,
> you can repeat steps 16-22
> instead of step 23, and
> continue repeating as many
> times as you want to make
> smaller branches.
> Such "infinitely foldable
> structure," also seen in
> *Conch* and other models
> later in the book, is one of
> the interesting aspect of the
> geometry of origami.

28 **29** **30**

Bring all four
points together.

The longest
branch is on top.

Leave a
small gap.

31 **32** **33** **34** **35**

The model should be
an isosceles triangle
when folded in step 35.

36 **37** **38** **39**

Crimp at the root of
the branch.

Outside reverse-fold

Crimp at the root of
the branch.

Finished. Make
the model stand
by itself.

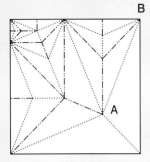

B

A

Theorems about creases

If you unfold *Tree* in step 30, you will see on the white side of the paper the crease pattern shown on the left. Note that the model was folded flat with these creases. Using this crease pattern as an example, let's examine some of the general features of flat-foldable creases.

Pay attention to the "corners" where mountain and valley creases meet. (Ignore those on the edges of the sheet for now.) You may find that:

1. The difference between the number of mountain and valley creases is always 2. (Maekawa Theorem)
2. If you add all angles between creases, one by one with alternate signs, the sum is always 0. (Kawasaki Theorem)

For example, look at the point A in the crease pattern. It has 2 mountain and 4 valley creases, so the difference is 2. The angles between the creases counter-clockwise from the right are 112.5°, 22.5°, 22.5°, 45°, 45°, and 112.5°. 112.5-22.5+22.5-45+45-112.5=0.

Though not all corners that satisfy these theorems are flat-foldable, all flat-foldable corners satisfy both of them. This is true not only in regular patterns like this but also patterns of crumpled and flattened sheets.

We can prove, from the Maekawa theorem, that any corner has an even number of creases. And that any crease pattern requires only two colors to paint the areas surrounded by the creases. One color represents all the areas facing up when folded, and the other all areas facing down.

If the model has one-sidedness (see *Orizuru Transformation*), as in this crease pattern, the corners on the edges also satisfy both of the theorems. For example, look at the point B. You can easily see that the Kawasaki theorem is satisfied. Now, imagine that the two edges fuse into one valley crease when folded, and the Maekawa theorem is also satisfied.

Keys to prove the theorems

Calculate the sum of interior angles of the polygon.

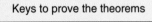

Mountain = 360°
Valley = 0°

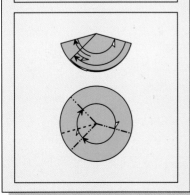

In the next section...

That concludes **fundamental models** and **simple models**. There is, however, no objective standards for complexity levels in origami, and you may think the models presented so far are not simple, as they are accompanied with complicated theories. In fact, they are not necessarily easier to fold than those in **intermediate models**.

Before we step forward to **intermediate models**, I want to introduce some models that break the "basic rules" of origami.

The "basic rule" is described as "one square sheet without cuts." Such origami is often thought to be "genuine" as in the title of this book.

However, there are many truly origami-like designs that are folded from shapes other than a square, with more than one sheet, or with cuts.

These models make us rethink about "authenticity" in origami.

Chapter 3
Varieties of Origami

"There is nothing in this world constant, but inconstancy."
Jonathan Swift

Hina dolls

Theme: Multi-piece
An example of model that is folded using multiple sheets. The purpose of this model is to use multiple colors.

Fujiyama Module

Theme: Modular
An example of modular origami, in which a lot of simple modules are assembled mainly into geometric shapes.

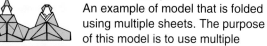
Tea-bag Reindeer

Theme: Irregular shape
Introduces a model folded using a sheet with an extremely odd shape. Origami paper does not have to be square.

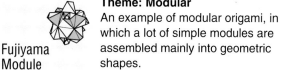
Connected Cranes, Kotobuki

Theme: Cut
Some models are more origami than kirigami or paper-craft, even though they are folded with cuts.

Hina dolls

Theme: Multi-piece
Fold using 6" (15 cm) origami paper.

This model breaks the rule of "one sheet" in "one square sheet without cuts."

A Bird base has four long flaps, which are not enough to make, say, a quadruped animal that has a head, a tail, and four legs.

One solution for this situation is to combine two Bird bases, as shown on the right. Although it expands the possibility of design without introducing difficult steps, it is not likely to offer puzzle-like twists. Generally speaking, however, using multiple sheets is not necessarily boring.

When we use multiple sheets, we can obtain not only more flaps but also more colors. Even with one sheet, we can use two colors. Using the inside-out technique, as in Santa Claus, we can use the colors of each side of the sheet. But with multiple sheets, we can use more than two colors.

This model is based on such idea. At the same time, I wanted to use as little colors as possible. So, I used a limited number of colors by making hair and hakama (Japanese traditional trousers) with one sheet.

Speaking of colors, we sometimes use decorated or painted paper. It is interesting to fold using such paper, especially for simple models, because we often get surprised with unexpected patterns appearing on finished models. A pair of artists Cochae explores a new genre of such origami called "graphic origami."

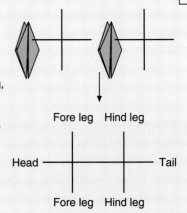

Designing a quadruped animal using two Bird bases.

Kimono for Male doll

Two sheets for each of Male and Female dolls

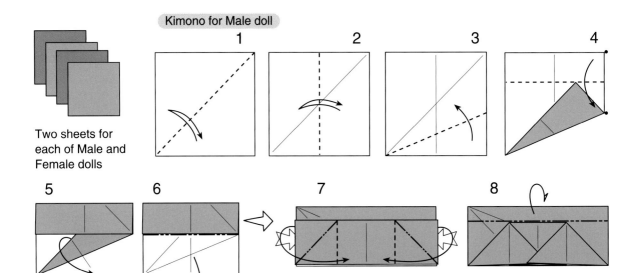

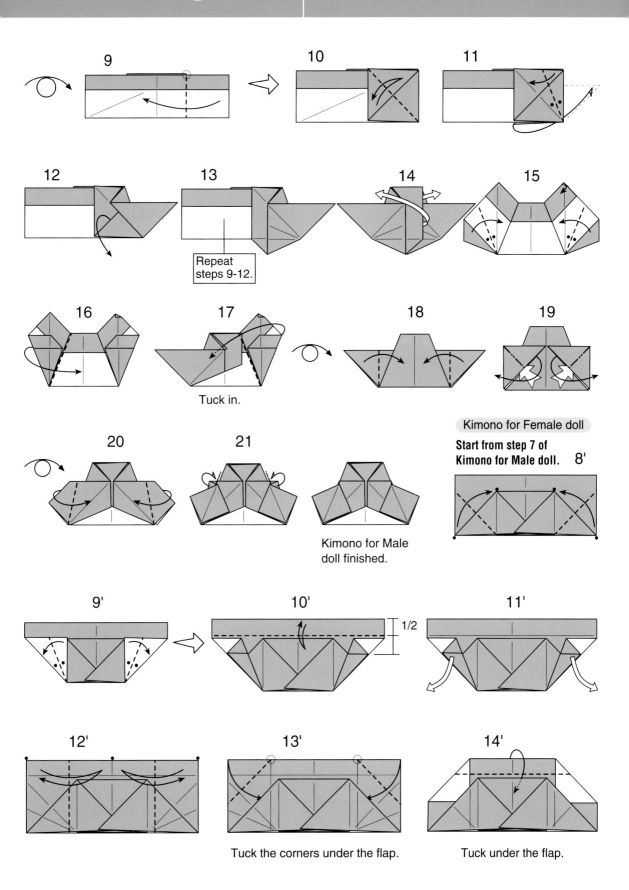

9

10

11

12

13

Repeat
steps 9-12.

14

15

16

17

Tuck in.

18

19

Kimono for Female doll

**Start from step 7 of
Kimono for Male doll.**   8'

20

21

Kimono for Male
doll finished.

9'

10'

1/2

11'

12'

Tuck the corners under the flap.

13'

14'

Tuck under the flap.

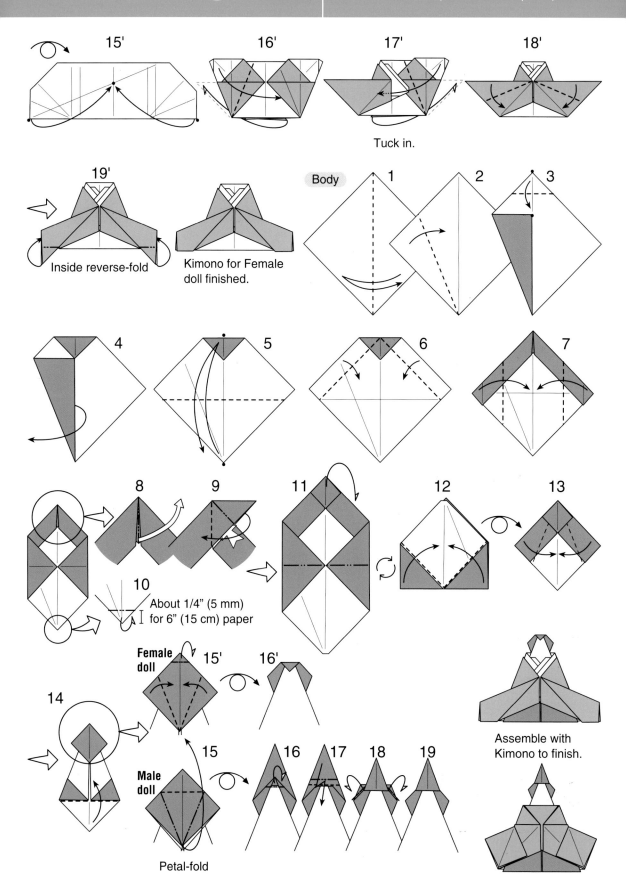

15'

16'

17'

18'

Tuck in.

19'

Inside reverse-fold

Kimono for Female doll finished.

Body

1

2

3

4

5

6

7

8

9

10

About 1/4" (5 mm)
for 6" (15 cm) paper

11

12

13

14

Female doll

15'

16'

Male doll

15

Petal-fold

16

17

18

19

Assemble with Kimono to finish.

Fujiyama Module

Theme: Modular

Fold using 6" (15 cm) origami paper cut into eight equal parts.

This model is an example of **modular origami**, where we use more sheets than "one square sheet without cuts."

Modular Origami

Modular Origami is a kind of multi-piece origami.

Many people have been creating a number of models of various shapes, each of which is usually assembled from identical modules. Although there are some traditional modular model such as the *Kusudama* (decorative ball), the notion of modular origami was first introduced by Kunihiko Kasahara who was interested in diverse variations of *Color Box* designed by Mitsunobu Sonobe. Besides using multiple sheets, typical modular models have the following features.

1. Each module is relatively simple.
2. No glue is required to assemble.
3. No new fold is required to assemble.
4. Modules can be assembled in different ways.

This model *Fujiyama Module* has all the features above. The most common way to assemble modules is to tuck a flap of a module into a pocket of another. But in this model, a half-open flap is wrapped over by another. It is sometimes puzzling to assemble in this way because the model tends to fall apart in the course of assembly, though it gets stable when completely assembled.

Use three or more sheets of 1 : 2 rectangle. (Cutting a 6" origami paper into eight parts is suggested.)

1

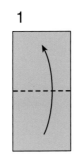

2

3

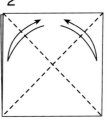

Fold and unfold the top layer only.

4

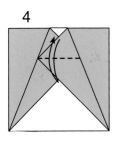

5

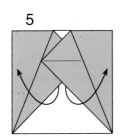

6

Repeat steps 2-6.

7

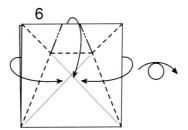

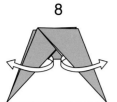

8

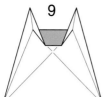

9

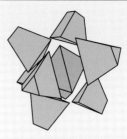

The structure of 12-piece #2 (a regular octahedron)

You may have to reverse this crease into mountain in some assembled models.

Finished.

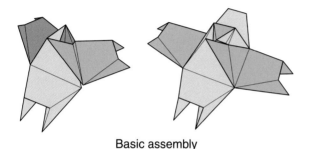

Basic assembly

To grasp the structures, imagine adding a pyramidal frustum to each face of a polyhedron whose faces are equilateral triangles, squares, or other polygons (see also *Chick* in **Complex Models**).

In addition, think about the symmetry of colors.

Note that the stability of the some assembled models varies depending on the stacking order of the layers.

Although 15 variations of assembled models are shown below, other combinations with 11, 13-23, 25-29, 31 and more pieces are also possible. Regardless of the number of modules, all faces of the underlying polyhedron are flat.

3-piece

4-piece

5-piece

6-piece #1

6-piece #2 (not stable)

7-piece (not stable)

8-piece

9-piece #1

9-piece #2

10-piece

12-piece #1

12-piece #2

24-piece

30-piece

30-piece #2 (reversed; not stable)

Tea-bag Reindeer

Theme: Irregular shape
Fold using a tea-bag envelope.

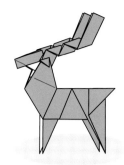

This model starts from nowhere near the "square" required in "one square sheet without cuts."

Shapes of paper

Why square is regarded as a special shape in origami?
There had been several discussions on a Web BBS several years ago, and here is the summary.

* History
    There is a enormous repertory of models that start from a square, including *Orizuru* (crane).
    Square origami paper has been commercialized and is now wide-spread.
    Obeying the rule leads to development of techniques, challenge, and unexpectedness.

* Simplicity
    Square is easy to make (and cut).
    Square is easy to describe.
    Square seems to be a tabula rasa in origami, as it resembles to almost nothing.

* Perfection
    Square is regarded as a prototypical shape. Square is regarded as a natural shape.

* Other geometric features
    Square is "symmetric" in a broad sense, because of its repeating structure and other reasons.
    Square has two types of axis of symmetry, a diagonal and a perpendicular bisectors, both of which offers different "expressions."

There are so many various factors that I do not dare to come to a conclusion. But I am sure square will continue dominating origami.

However, as I said at the beginning of this book, many sheets of paper around us are not square.

The most common shape worldwide is the rectangle with 1.414... (~√2) : 1 aspect ratio, which is also called silver ratio. This shape has been standardized because the ratio of its half shape is the same. This property is also useful in origami. Some traditional models such as airplanes and boxes start from that or similar rectangles. One can say that the silver rectangle is a close relative of the square, because the length of the long side is the same of the diagonal of a square whose sides are equal to the short side.

Besides the rectangle, various shapes such as a rectangle with the golden ratio or 1 : 1.618..., a tape, and all kinds of polygon can be used in origami. Bank notes, with ratio of about 1 : 2, are also common in origami. In short, sheets of any shape can be used in origami as long as the main method of design is folding.

Silver rectangle	1

1.414..

Golden rectangle	1

1.618..

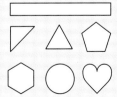

Various shapes

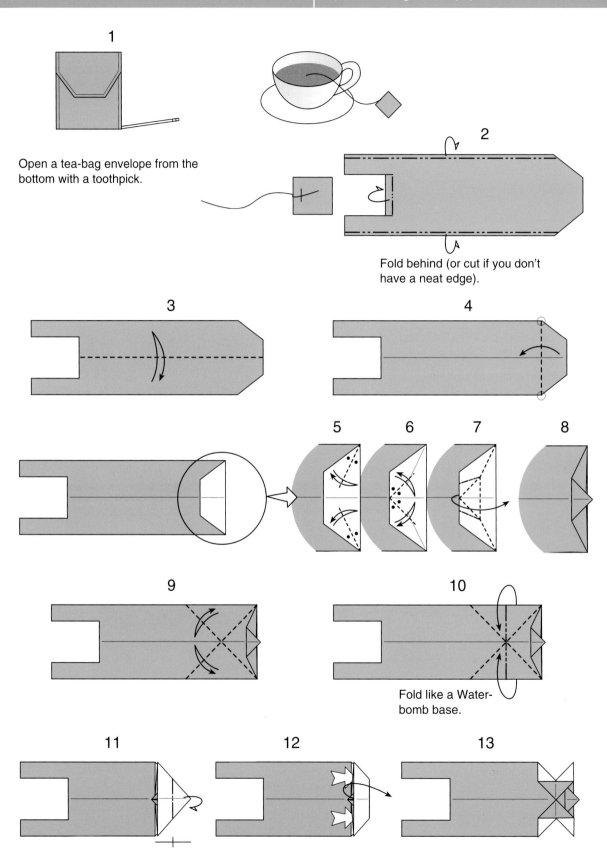

1

Open a tea-bag envelope from the bottom with a toothpick.

2

Fold behind (or cut if you don't have a neat edge).

3

4

5 **6** **7** **8**

9

10

Fold like a Water-bomb base.

11 **12** **13**

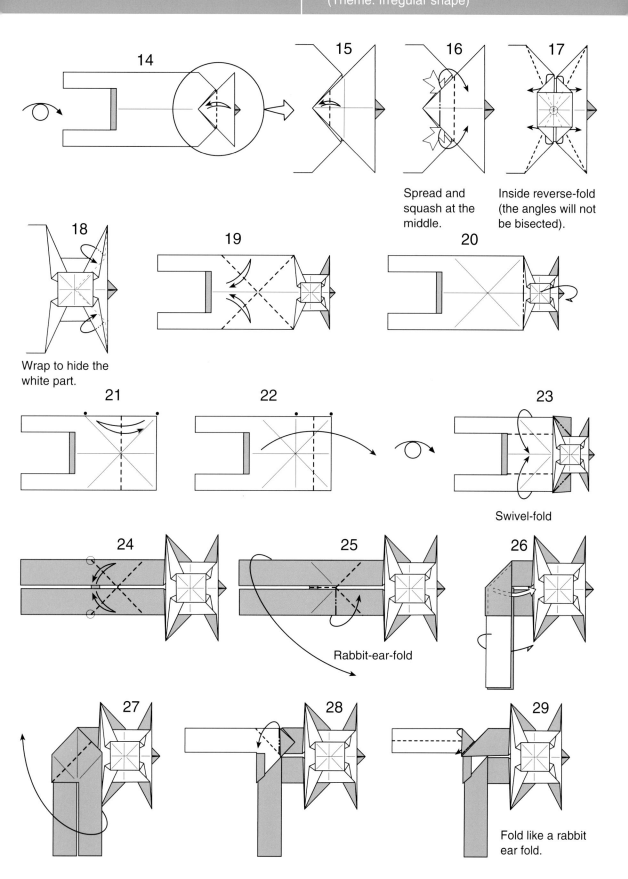

16 Spread and squash at the middle.

17 Inside reverse-fold (the angles will not be bisected).

18 Wrap to hide the white part.

23 Swivel-fold

25 Rabbit-ear-fold

29 Fold like a rabbit ear fold.

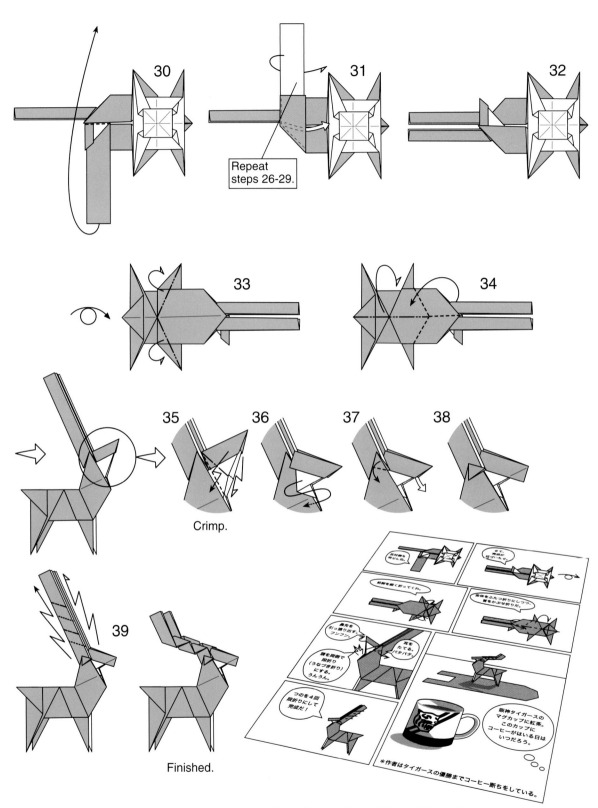

30

31

Repeat
steps 26-29.

32

33

34

35

36

37

38

Crimp.

39

Finished.

Sample page from *Origami Tanteidan
Convention Book volume 3*
(1997, self-publication, out-of-print)

Connected Cranes, Kotobuki

Theme: Cut
Fold using washi
(Japanese handmade paper).

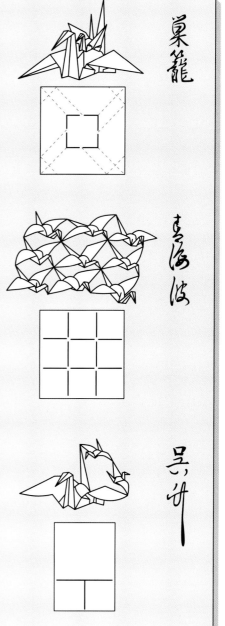

> Let's think about "without cuts" as in "one square sheet without cuts" based on a model with some cuts.

Cuts in *Sembazuru Orikata*

In 1797, Rito Akisato, who was known for his *Miyako Meisho Zue (Pictures of Landmarks in Kyoto)*, published a book of kyoka (comic haiku) titled *Hiden Sembazuru Orikata*. The book contains 49 models of connected-crane designed by Gido, who was the chief priest of Choenji temple at Kuwana city, under the pen name of Rokoan.

This book has a big historic value as the oldest known book of recreational origami (versus ceremonial origami). In addition, the models in the book are still attractive today even though they are more than 200 years old.

Although each crane is just an ordinary traditional *Orizuru*, the connections of cranes are as interesting as puzzles and filled with surprises. Some examples from the book are shown on this page, *Sugomori*, *Seigaiha*, *Kuretake*, and *Imosemaya*.

The book contains no folding diagrams but cutting patterns and pictures of finished models. Although they include many cuts, all the models adhere to two rules:

1. Start from a rectangle (including square) sheet.
2. Do not cut off any part.

Japanese traditional origami (then called "orikata" or "orisue") was different from modern origami in that cuts were not avoided. Nevertheless, the models of *Sembazuru Orikata* are still popular origami even now.

That is because, in my opinion, the models are geometric and puzzle-like. Moreover, even if they includes cuts, the main sequences still consist of folds, and cuts are subsequent to folds.

By the way, such connected-crane models were traditionally called "sembazuru," or literally one-thousand cranes. But more recently the Japanese call it "renkaku" or "renzuru."

Cuts in origami

Some say cuts are prohibited in origami. But if cuts are really prohibited, we must use paper that has no border, such as an infinitely wide plane or a sphere. We can only obtain a square sheet by cuts. Moreover, cutting relates to the number of sheets used for a multi-piece model.

For example, instead of starting from two square sheets, one can start from one sheet of 1 : 2 rectangle and cut it in half.

Of course, cutting also closely relates to the shape of paper. For example, the picture on the right is the shape for *Crab*, appearing in a private encyclopedia of 19th century titled *Kayaragusa*, which contains historic records of origami. At first glance, it looks nothing but a square with cuts. But we can also say it is a hexadecagon with four 360° angle corners and twelve right angle corners. That is, we can say this model is folded using one hexadecagon sheet without cuts.

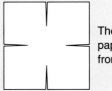

The shape of paper for Crab from Kayaragusa.

For me, the home of origami is still in a square without cuts. But, in a broader perspective, my criteria of "origami-like" is how elegant the model is in a geometric sense.

From that point of view, models in *Sembazuru Orikata* are truly origami-like. The rule of "one rectangle sheet without cuts-off" is as well elaborated as "one square sheet without cuts."

Here is my connected-crane model that I believe Rokoan did not come up with. To avoid cuts-off, you must fold smaller and smaller cranes infinitely. But in reality, it will be impossible to fold more than five or six.

It is titled *Kotobuki* because it resembles to the kanji character for "kotobuki" (long life or celebration). I think it is also reminiscent of the chain of generations because of its infinite repetition, and that it is associated with cranes flying by Mount Fuji in a picture of Rosetsu Nagasawa.

Steps 1-4 constructs the golden ratio Φ (phi) = 1.618... = $(\sqrt{5} + 1) / 2$ by folding a square.

It is easier to measure with a ruler, though.

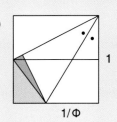

1/Φ

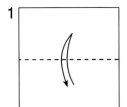

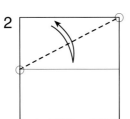

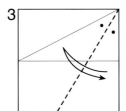

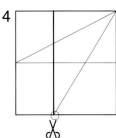

1.618..

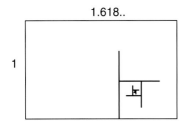

Cut up to the middle of the side of the smaller square.

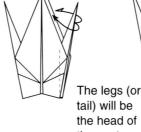

The legs (or tail) will be the head of the next crane.

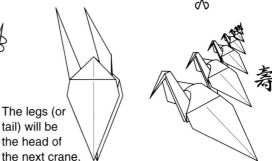

Gift Box

Theme: Iso-area
In this model, the front and back sides of paper are folded almost identically.

Papillon

Theme: Composition of points
Compares the composition of points with that of *Wild Boar* to show the basics of technical folding and origami design.

Standing Crane

Theme: Technical folding
Explains technical folding from a practical point of view by analyzing the crease pattern of this model.

Sheep

Theme: Why from a square?
Ponders about origami design derived from a square shape by the crease pattern examination.

Squid

Theme: Axis of symmetry
Examines two types of axis of symmetry of the square, i.e. diagonal and parallel lines.

Three-headed Crane

Theme: Technical folding; Preparation
Explains how to construct a crease pattern from a sketch of branches. Also explains the idea of preparation.

Cow

Theme: Pig base
Explains features of the Pig base and their importance as the basics of technical folding.

Western Dragon

Theme: Y-pattern
An example of model that has many instances of Y-shaped crease pattern.

Chapter 4

Intermediate Models

"Everything should be made as simple as possible, but no simpler."
Albert Einstein

Horse

Theme: Geometric construction
Shows that paper-folding can be used to replace a straight-edge and compass in folding landmarks.

Rabbit

Theme: Solid body
Illustrates some methods of making three-dimensional origami models.

Devil Mask

Theme: Variation
As a variation of *Tiger Mask*, this model provides a typical example of how one model is modified into another.

Frog

Theme: Approximation
This model makes use of the approximation $5 \times \sqrt{2} - 3 \fallingdotseq 4$. Explains the difference between origami and pure geometry, where lines have no width and planes have no thickness.

Triceratops

Theme: Open-back, Open-belly
Explains the notion of open-back and open-belly as one of the origami design styles.

Tiger Mask

Theme: Polyhedron
Explains a basic technique to make three-dimensional models using polyhedra.

Penguin

Theme: 15 degrees; Cone
This model is based on 15° angle or one sixth of the right angle. Also examines curved surfaces that can be made from a flat surface.

Pyramid

Theme: Infinite folding
An example of model that can be folded in the same pattern infinitely until the physical limitations of the paper.

Gift Box

Theme: Iso-area
Fold using 6" (15 cm) origami paper.

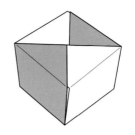

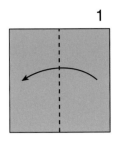

2 **3** **4** **5**

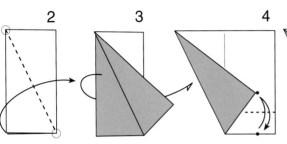

Pinch at the edge.

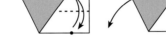

Steps 1-5 are the sequence to accurately divide a side into five. You can confirm it in steps 6-8.

The key to prove this construction. The ratio of the sides of two gray triangles is 3 : 4 : 5.

6

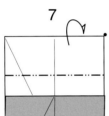

Extend the crease made in step 4.

7 **8** **9** **10**

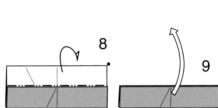

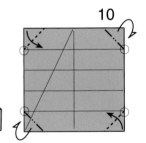

11 **12** **13** **14**

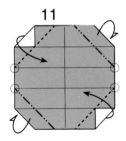

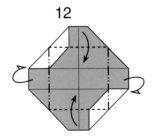

Fold according to the sequence indicated.

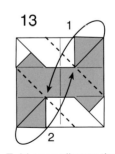

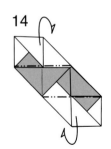

15 **16** **17** **18**

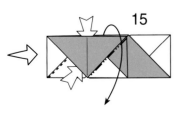

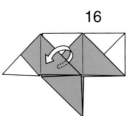

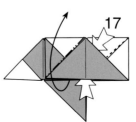

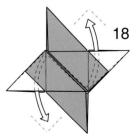

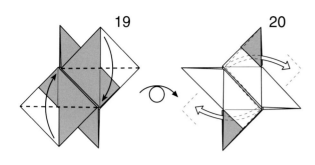

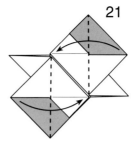

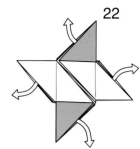

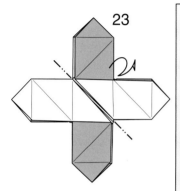

Iso-area

The model is iso-area in steps 18 and 23. In other words, the creases are identical at the front and back sides of paper. The notion of iso-area folding was introduced by Toshikazu Kawasaki with his *Iso-area Cube* and some other examples. It corresponds to **rotoinversion symmetry** in crystallography. The word "rotoinversion" comes from "rotation and inversion." Note that inversion corresponds in origami to reversing mountain and valley folds and rotating 180°. This model is also an example of **twist folding**, coined by Shuzo Fujimoto.

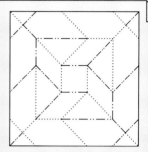

The crease pattern on step 23 will be the same if you reverse mountain and valley creases and rotate.

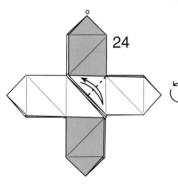

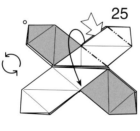

Make a half cube.

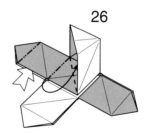

Make a half cube inside.

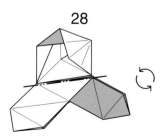

Mountain-fold on the center

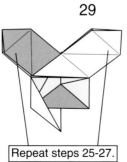

Repeat steps 25-27.

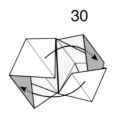

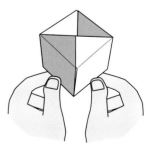

To finish, pinch firmly all eight edges so that the cube does not open.

Squid

Theme: Axis of symmetry

Fold using 6" (15 cm) origami paper.

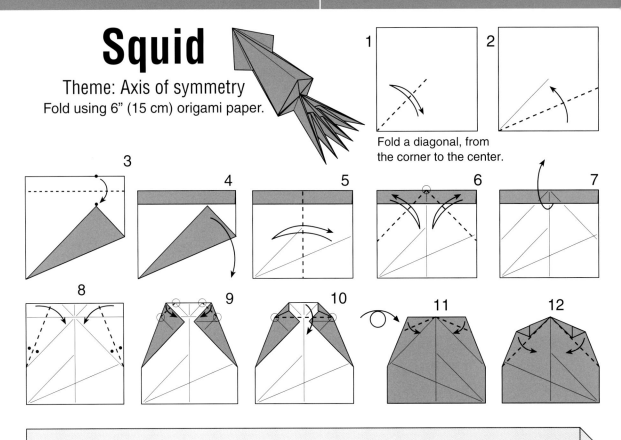

1

2

Fold a diagonal, from the corner to the center.

3

4

5

6

7

8

9

10

11

12

Axis of symmetry of the square

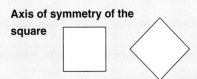

The square on the right looks larger, although they have the same area.

You may have seen the illusion created by the same square which looks different when placed "horizontally" or "diagonally." Not only the area but also the shape itself often looks different, to a point that the shape on the right is sometimes called diamond instead of square.

In other words, the square has two different facets. That is the reason for the general attraction of the use of the square for origami. When designing models, the first thing we decide is, in most cases, the axis of symmetry, which is usually either a diagonal line or a line parallel to the side. The decision is both annoying and enjoyable for designers. (I said "usually" because some models have asymmetric structures, as in *Snake*, or structures of rotation or rotoinversion symmetry, as in *Gift Box*.)

The notion of axis of symmetry is also useful when modifying existing models. One example is the use of the blintz fold as in *Elephant*, and this *Squid* is a derivative example of that.

First I designed *Carrot*, which is basically a pyramid with leaves. Since it also looked like a squid for me, I wanted to add fins to make it closer to a real squid. At the same time, I wanted to keep the crease pattern intact because it already was a high quality design. So I rotated it 45° and placed it in a larger square. Then I found a crease pattern that offered fins in the right position.

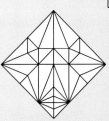

The crease pattern of *Carrot* (mountain and valley folds are not shown).

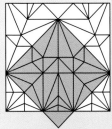

The crease pattern of *Squid* (mountain and valley folds are not shown).
The gray area is the same to the *Carrot*.

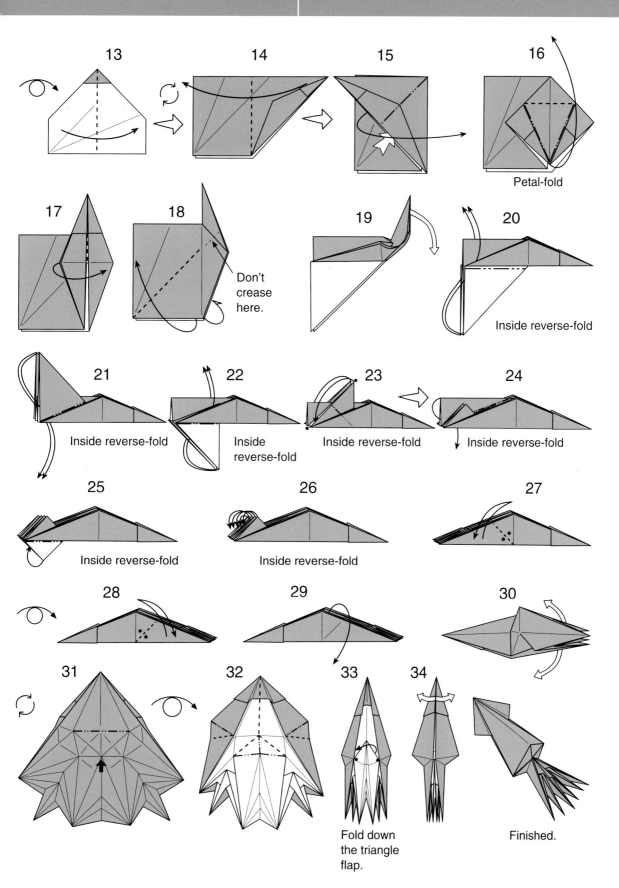

13

14

15

16

Petal-fold

17

18

Don't crease here.

19

20

Inside reverse-fold

21

Inside reverse-fold

22

Inside reverse-fold

23

Inside reverse-fold

24

Inside reverse-fold

25

Inside reverse-fold

26

Inside reverse-fold

27

28

29

30

31

32

33

Fold down the triangle flap.

34

Finished.

Papillon (Dog)

Theme: Composition of points
Fold using 6" (15 cm) origami paper.

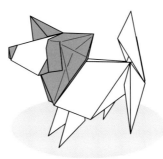

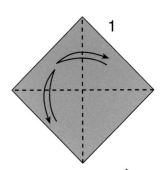

1

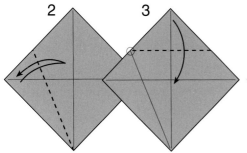

2   3

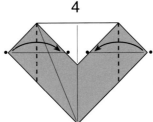

4

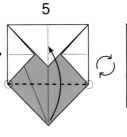

5

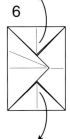

6

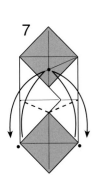

7

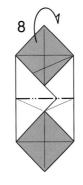

8

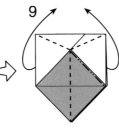

9

Fold like a rabbit ear fold.

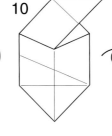

10

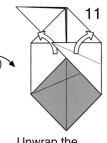

11

Unwrap the interlocked layers.

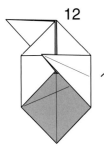

12

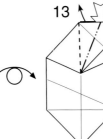

13

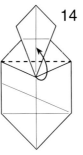

14

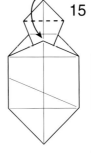

15

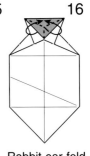

16

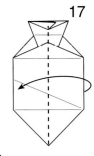

17

Rabbit-ear-fold

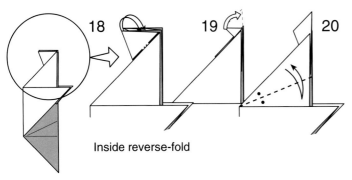

18   19   20

Inside reverse-fold

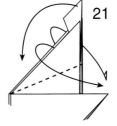

21

Fold like an outside reverse fold.

22

Repeat behind.

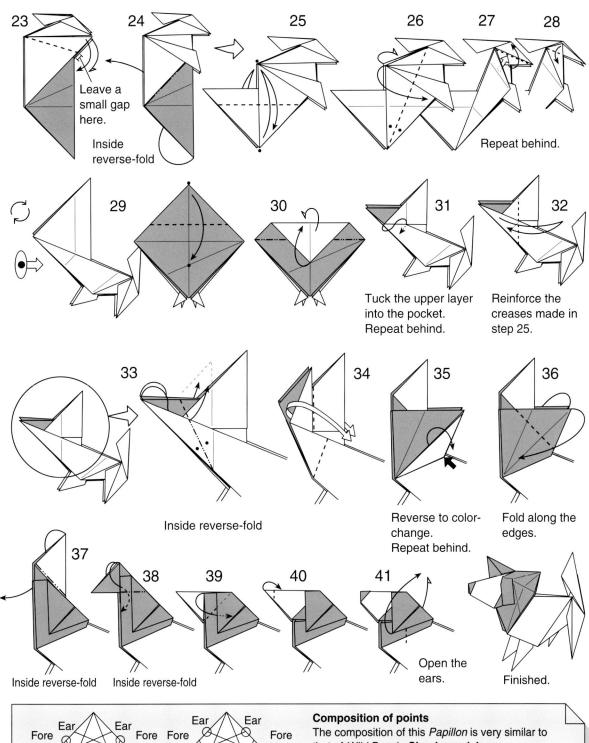

23 Leave a small gap here.

Inside reverse-fold

24

25

26 Repeat behind.

27

28

29

30

31 Tuck the upper layer into the pocket. Repeat behind.

32 Reinforce the creases made in step 25.

33 Inside reverse-fold

34

35 Reverse to color-change. Repeat behind.

36 Fold along the edges.

37 Inside reverse-fold

38 Inside reverse-fold

39

40

41 Open the ears.

Finished.

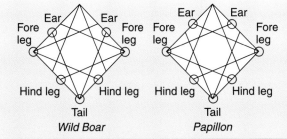

	Ear		Ear	
Fore leg				Fore leg
Hind leg				Hind leg
		Tail		

Wild Boar

Papillon

Composition of points

The composition of this *Papillon* is very similar to that of *Wild Boar* in **Simple models**.

They are different only in the position of the ears and the nose. So, this means, you can design other quadruped animals by modifying *Wild Boar* or *Papillon*.

In fact, I designed other breeds of dogs and other animals like a cat from their variations.

Three-headed Crane

Theme: Technical folding; Preparation
Fold using 6" (15 cm) origami paper.

> The idea of this model came from a mystery novel called *Tokeikan-no Satsujin (Homicide of Clock Pavilion)* by Yukito Ayatsuji, where a character folds a three-headed crane. But the model only existed inside the author's head at the time of the writing.

Basics of technical folding and preparation

A square has only four corners. However, we need six flaps to make a three-headed crane, for its two wings, three heads, and one tail (or one flap for both legs). The stick figure on the right represents the required flaps. Although *Papillon* has eight flaps, a head, two ears, four legs, and a tail, they are too short to be used for the crane. So, how can we do it?

The basic tree figure for a three-headed crane

The easiest solution is to start from a hexagon. But that will be against the "one square sheet without cuts" rule.

Starting from a hexagon?

Another solution is to prepare extra points in a square, such as using the blintz fold.

Start from a square, fold in half to make an isosceles right triangle, and make it square again by assembling the three corners together. Then we have four points on one corner of the square that are prepared for three heads. But, if we fold a Bird base with the prepared square and unfold, we can see that the crease pattern consists of four Bird bases. Re-arranging these creases, we will obtain nine long flaps. This pattern is more suitable for an insect with six legs, a head, a thorax, and an abdomen, than a three-headed crane.

A prepared square

The crease pattern of Bird base from the prepared square (mountain and valley folds are not shown).

So, there should be a more efficient pattern that offers six flaps of the same length from a square.
Toshiyuki Meguro, Fumiaki Kawahata, and Robert Lang developed a design method called circle-packing. In the crease pattern of *Papillon*, I put circles only to indicate the places of points, not the length.
One can indicate the length of points with the radii of circles, because a flap requires an area of circle whose center is at the tip of it and whose radius equals to its length. Kawahata explained it by an intuitive analogy of an umbrella, that the radius of an umbrella equals to its length when folded. Note that a flap requires only a half or a quarter of the circle if the center is on the edge of paper.

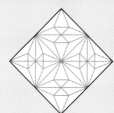

Base from the above crease pattern
It has nine long flaps.

The circle packing on the right, for example, gives six flaps. From it, we can fold a Bird base that has six flaps. And the base is larger than that from the prepared square above. Note that two of the four corners of the square will be folded inside and will not become points in the finished model.
That means, the model can be folded from a hexagon that is inscribed in a square (shown on the right). Now, we have come back to the first idea of starting from a hexagon, but this hexagon is easier to fold from a square.

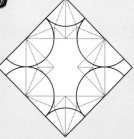

Six circles packed in a square, each of which corresponding to a flap. Gray lines are part of the crease pattern.

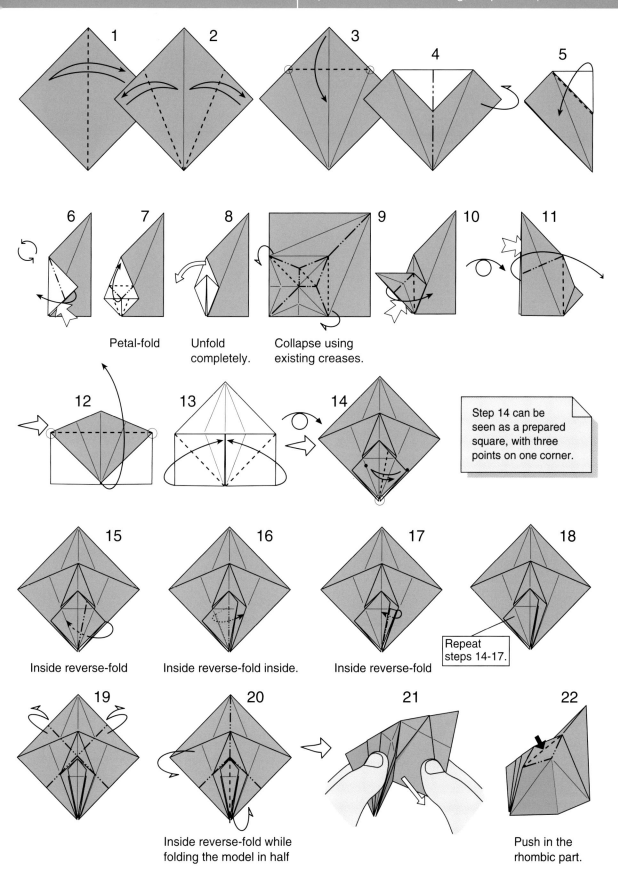

Petal-fold

Unfold completely.

Collapse using existing creases.

Step 14 can be seen as a prepared square, with three points on one corner.

Inside reverse-fold

Inside reverse-fold inside.

Inside reverse-fold

Repeat steps 14-17.

Inside reverse-fold while folding the model in half

Push in the rhombic part.

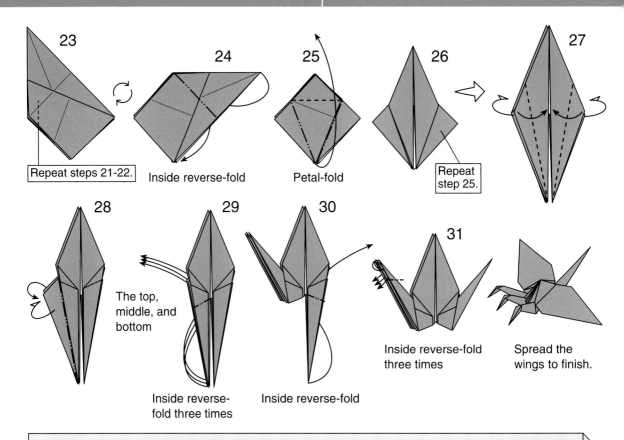

23 Repeat steps 21-22.

24 Inside reverse-fold

25 Petal-fold

26 Repeat step 25.

27

28

29 The top, middle, and bottom — Inside reverse-fold three times

30 Inside reverse-fold

31 Inside reverse-fold three times

Spread the wings to finish.

Basics of technical folding: "Molecule"

I have said that the length of a flap corresponds to the radius of the circle in technical folding. I also introduced circles inscribed in a triangle in *Orizuru Transformation* in **Fundamental Models**. Though it may be confusing, these two types of circle are different. They intersect with each other at a right angle, as shown on the right.

From a different point of view, the radius of the inscribed circle can be seen as the length of obtuse "flap," or the "width" of the flap in the original orientation.

An area with a set of related creases, such as in the "rabbit ear fold of isosceles right triangle" on the right, is sometimes called **molecule**, term created by Toshiyuki Meguro who was inspired by my notion of **atom**, which is an area without creases, such as the triangles shown in *Wild Boar*.

Origami molecules can be polymerized just as in Chemistry. A unit molecule is called monomer, and a compound of small number (2-100) of monomers is called oligomer. "Oligo-," as in oligosaccharide, means "a few." Plastics is compound of more molecules and called polymer, as "poly-" means "many."

If a rabbit ear fold were a monomer, a Bird base would be an oligomer because it consists of four monomers. Why don't we call it oligami? Then, a super-complex model, such as *Ryujin* or Eastern Dragon designed by Satoshi Kamiya with all its scales, would be called a polygami. Even though it consists of so many molecules, the model is still a developable combination of developable units. By the way, be careful to spell this pun correctly, as "polygamy" means plural marriage.

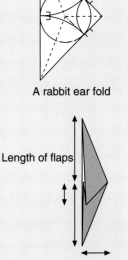

A rabbit ear fold

Length of flaps

Width

Standing Crane

Theme: Technical folding

Fold using 6" (15 cm) origami paper. Thin washi (Japanese handmade paper) larger than 8" (20 cm) is better.

Standing Crane and practical technical folding

The subject of the previous model, Three-headed Crane, is rather eccentric. Its basic structure can be applied to a two-legged crane by just flipping the front and the back. However, the middle flap would be too long for the tail of the crane. We only need five long flaps, which can be obtained by the crease pattern on the right. It is the crease pattern of Standing Crane. The thin lines define the composition of points, and the thick lines (black and gray) represent the creases. Note that mountain and valley creases are not shown.

If you follow the thin lines, you can find river-like areas besides circles that correspond to flaps. Whereas a circle represents a branch, a river corresponds to a trunk that connects some branches. Compare the pattern with the tree figure on the right.

To understand the crease pattern, look at the areas surrounded by the thick black lines, or "molecules." Each area, except the two triangles at both ends that will be folded inside, will be folded so that all the sides are aligned, as the quadrangles discussed in Orizuru Transformation. Because of this special feature, called single-value by Toshiyuki Meguro or uniaxial by Robert Lang, we can easily combine many "molecules."

You may think that the trunk is too long for a structure of the crane. In fact, we can use a composition without rivers to obtain a tree without trunks. With such composition, however, it is difficult to arrange the angles of creases, and the flaps tend to have random shapes, even though they have desired lengths. Such a model is not likely to be easy to fold.

We can make an ordered structure with random angles by, for example, placing points on a grid. But arranging angles is one of the easiest ways to design clear and clean models. For this model, rather than taking care of the length of points, I arranged triangles and quadrangles with specific angles (such as those explained in Wild Boar), as if they are tiles, so that the entire crease pattern is flat-foldable. Actually, I came up with another pattern, which is shown on the right.

Just as Three-headed Crane can be folded from a hexagon, this model can be folded from a pentagon shown on the right, with one right-angled corner and four 67.5° corners.

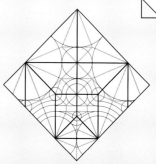

Composition of points and creases.

Circles represent flaps, and areas surrounded by thick black lines are "molecules."

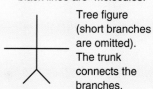

Tree figure (short branches are omitted). The trunk connects the branches.

Another crease pattern for five long points

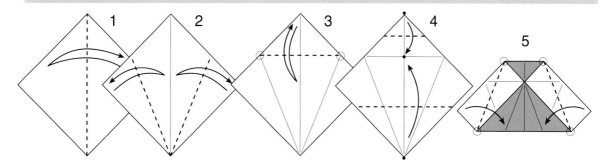

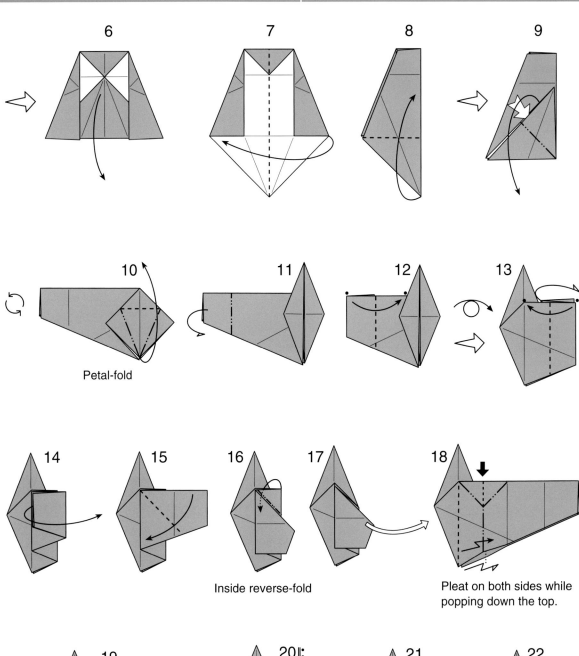

10 Petal-fold

16 Inside reverse-fold

18 Pleat on both sides while popping down the top.

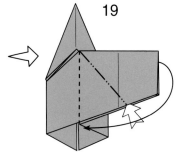

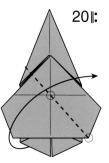

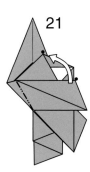

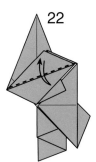

Pivot and rotate
so that the
corners will meet.

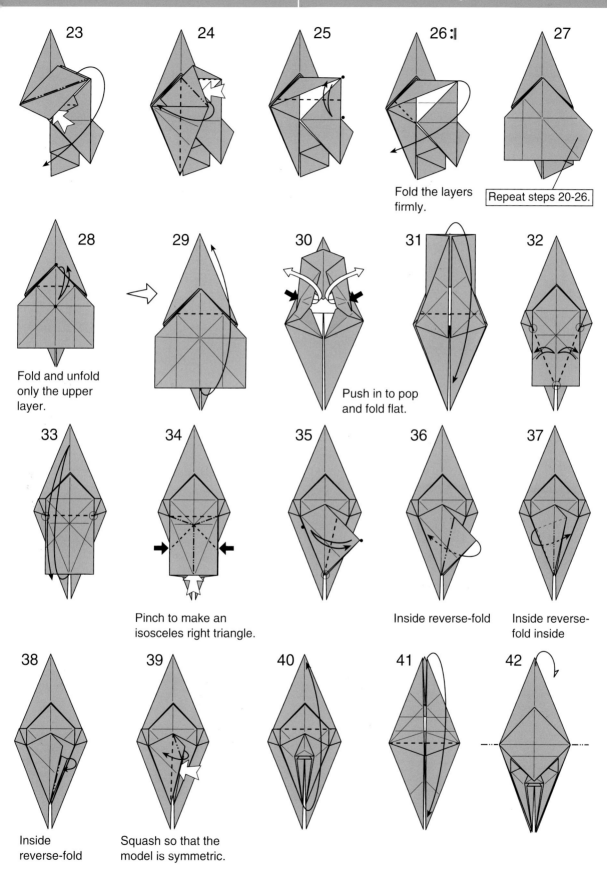

23 **24** **25** **26 :‖** **27**

Fold the layers firmly.

Repeat steps 20-26.

28
Fold and unfold only the upper layer.

29

30
Push in to pop and fold flat.

31

32

33

34
Pinch to make an isosceles right triangle.

35

36
Inside reverse-fold

37
Inside reverse-fold inside

38
Inside reverse-fold

39
Squash so that the model is symmetric.

40

41

42

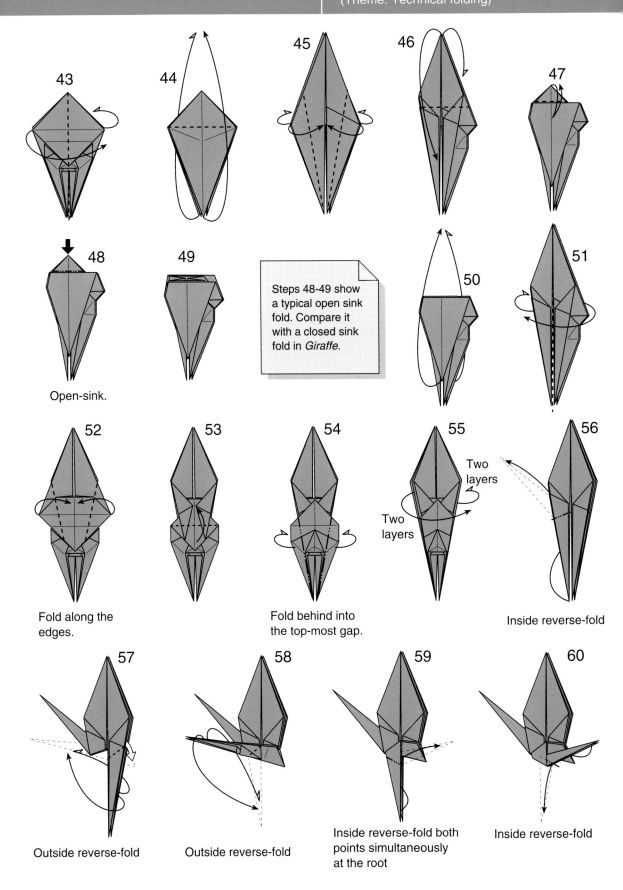

43

44

45

46

47

48

Open-sink.

49

Steps 48-49 show a typical open sink fold. Compare it with a closed sink fold in *Giraffe*.

50

51

52

Fold along the edges.

53

54

Fold behind into the top-most gap.

55

Two layers

Two layers

56

Inside reverse-fold

57

Outside reverse-fold

58

Outside reverse-fold

59

Inside reverse-fold both points simultaneously at the root

60

Inside reverse-fold

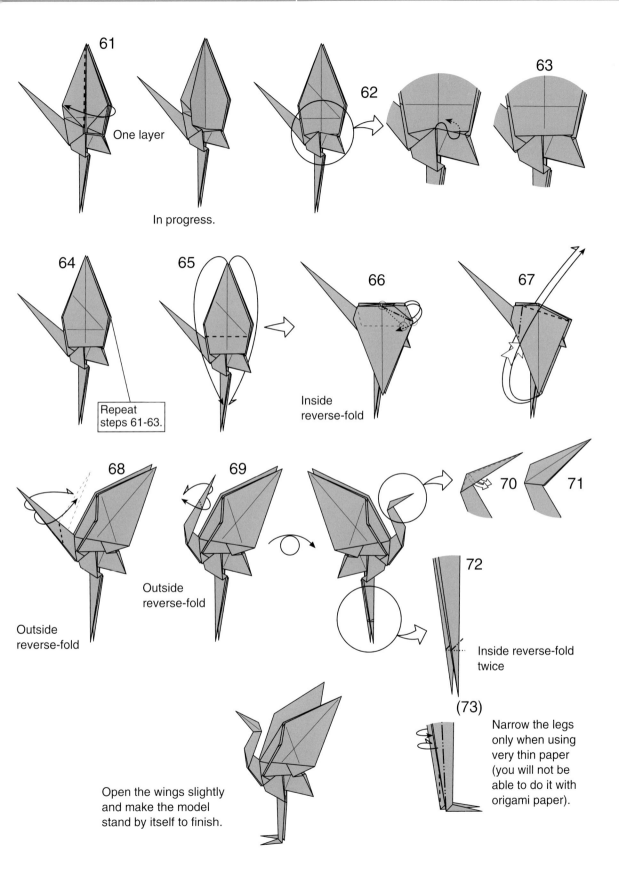

61

One layer

In progress.

62

63

64

Repeat
steps 61-63.

65

66

Inside
reverse-fold

67

68

Outside
reverse-fold

Outside
reverse-fold

69

Outside
reverse-fold

70   71

72

Inside reverse-fold
twice

(73)

Narrow the legs
only when using
very thin paper
(you will not be
able to do it with
origami paper).

Open the wings slightly
and make the model
stand by itself to finish.

Cow

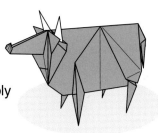

Theme: Pig base

Fold using 6" (15 cm) or preferably larger origami paper.

Step 5 shows a (blintzed) Pig base. Though it looks similar to traditional *Double Boat* (shown below), they are completely different.

Pig base

In *Standing Crane*, I explained the trunk in a tree structure. The base of traditional *Pig* shows a structure with a typical use of the trunk. The Pig base has a trunk in the middle and three branches at each end. You can see the central river in the circle-river diagram that corresponds to the trunk.

From the viewpoint of "molecules" or areas of grouped creases, the base consists of two quadrangular "molecules," that is, two 1 : 2 rectangular "molecules."

Now, let's take a closer look at quadrangular "molecules." Any quadrangle can be folded so that all edges align. (Robert Lang proved that it is true with any polygon, but here we examine only quadrangles.) For example, as explained in *Orizuru Transformation*, a quadrangle that has an inscribed circle can be folded as shown in the left and center picture in the middle row. The center quadrangle is folded in the same way as a Water-bomb base from a square. If we extend this pattern to a rectangle and other quadrangles, we must add a crease to make a trunk.

The crease pattern on the right is for Tiger I published before. Although it has more creases because it is based on 22.5° angles, you can see two 1 : 1.5 rectangle "molecules" next to each other. They define the basic structure, and the other parts create flaps for ears. So this pattern can be applied to different quadruped animals.

This *Cow* is also derived from a Pig base, though not from the crease pattern on the right. Before transformed in step 6, it starts with a blintzed Pig base (step 5).

The crease pattern of the Pig base.

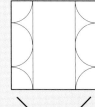

The tree figure of the Pig base.

Pig

Folding quadrangles to align all the edges. (The quadrangles on the left and center has an inscribed circle.)

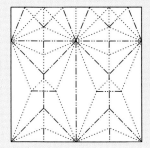

A crease pattern that can be used for the design of different animals.

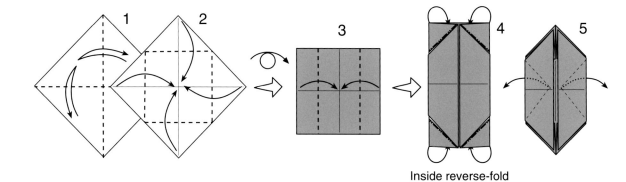

Inside reverse-fold

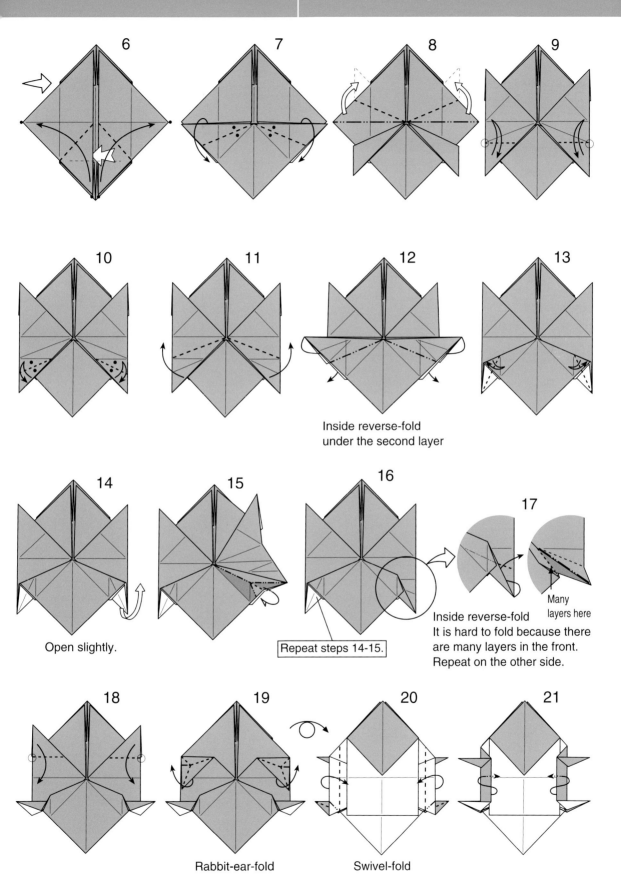

6 **7** **8** **9**

10 **11** **12** **13**

Inside reverse-fold
under the second layer

14 **15** **16** **17**

Open slightly.

Repeat steps 14-15.

Inside reverse-fold
It is hard to fold because there
are many layers in the front.
Repeat on the other side.

Many
layers here

18 **19** **20** **21**

Rabbit-ear-fold

Swivel-fold

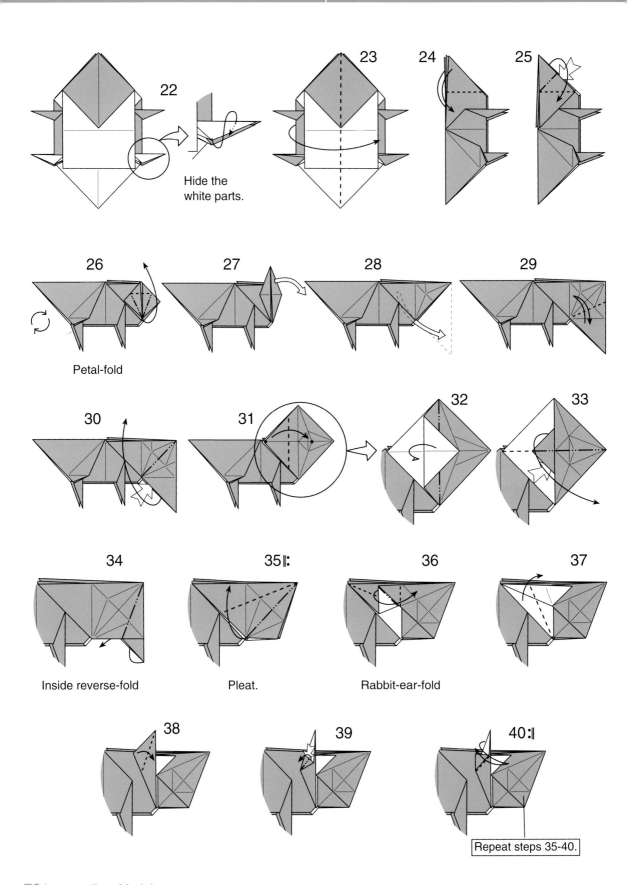

22 Hide the white parts.

23

24

25

26 Petal-fold

27

28

29

30

31

32

33

34 Inside reverse-fold

35 Pleat.

36 Rabbit-ear-fold

37

38

39

40 Repeat steps 35-40.

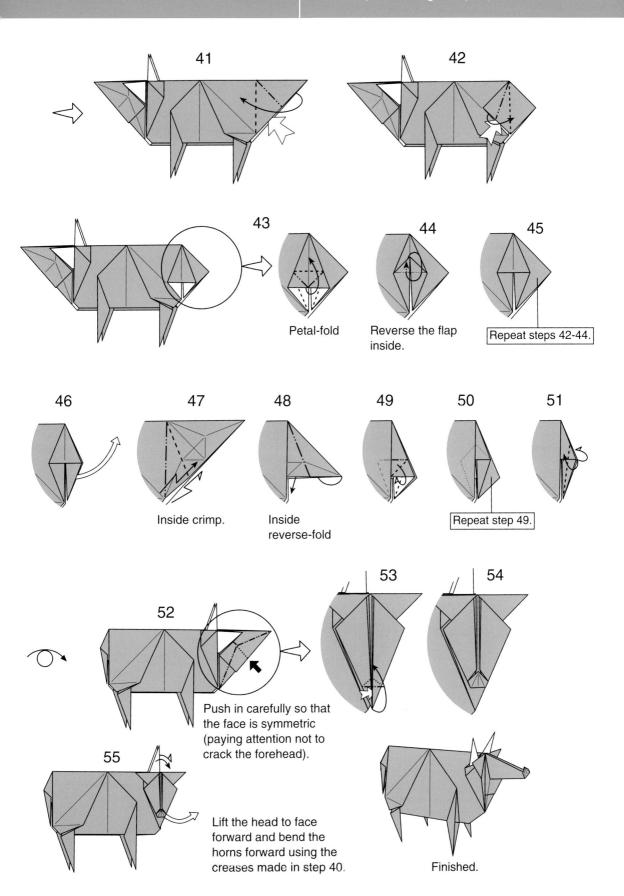

41

42

43

Petal-fold

44

Reverse the flap inside.

45

Repeat steps 42-44.

46

47

Inside crimp.

48

Inside reverse-fold

49

50

Repeat step 49.

51

52

Push in carefully so that the face is symmetric (paying attention not to crack the forehead).

53

54

55

Lift the head to face forward and bend the horns forward using the creases made in step 40.

Finished.

Sheep

Theme: Why from a square?
Fold using 6" (15 cm) origami paper.

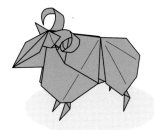

The crease pattern below looks like a lion head for me. I would say that is another instance of "mitate."

Why from a square?

The crease pattern of *Sheep* is shown on the right. You can see that none of four corners of the square is used for a point like a horn or a leg. This model can be folded from a hexagon inscribed in a square, just like *Three-headed Crane* can be folded from a hexagon and *Standing Crane* a pentagon.

Then, you may wonder if these models are really folded from squares. My answer is the following. First, as seen in *Three-headed Crane*, it is unexpectedly often the case that we can use a square more efficiently when we do not use corners for points. That puzzle-like unexpectedness is a significant part of origami. And it becomes more unexpected when we start from a "simple" shape of square.

Moreover, a design is based on and has an affinity to square if it requires a shape that can be easily derived from a square. It is natural to fold such a design using a square sheet, just the same as we do not fold *Orizuru* using the star shape shown on the right.

Which is true? That the creases harmonize with the square because we are using a square, or that the square is chosen as the handiest shape because we standardize angles and other aspects? I would say this is a chicken and egg question. Anyway, I strongly feel that the square is interesting and very rich.

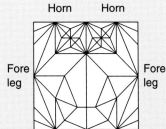

Horn   Horn

Fore leg   Fore leg

Hind leg   Hind leg

The crease pattern of *Sheep* (mountain and valley folds are not shown).

The basic structure of *Sheep*.

Orizuru can be folded using this shape.

1

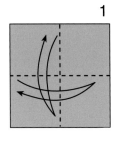

2

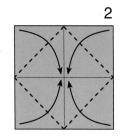

3

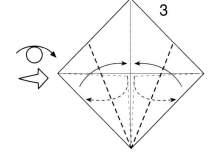

4

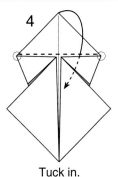

Tuck in.

5

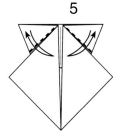

6

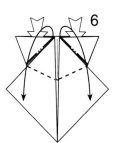

7

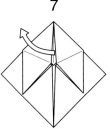

8

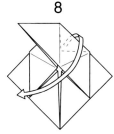

Step 8 shows a blintzed Little-bird base, folded with a different sequence from that in *Giraffe*.

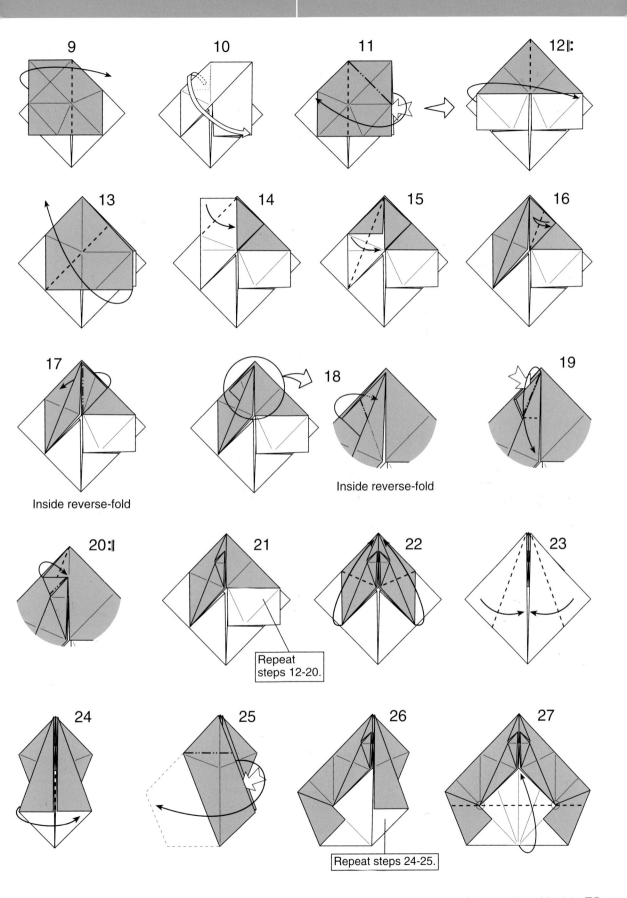

17 Inside reverse-fold

18 Inside reverse-fold

Repeat steps 12-20.

Repeat steps 24-25.

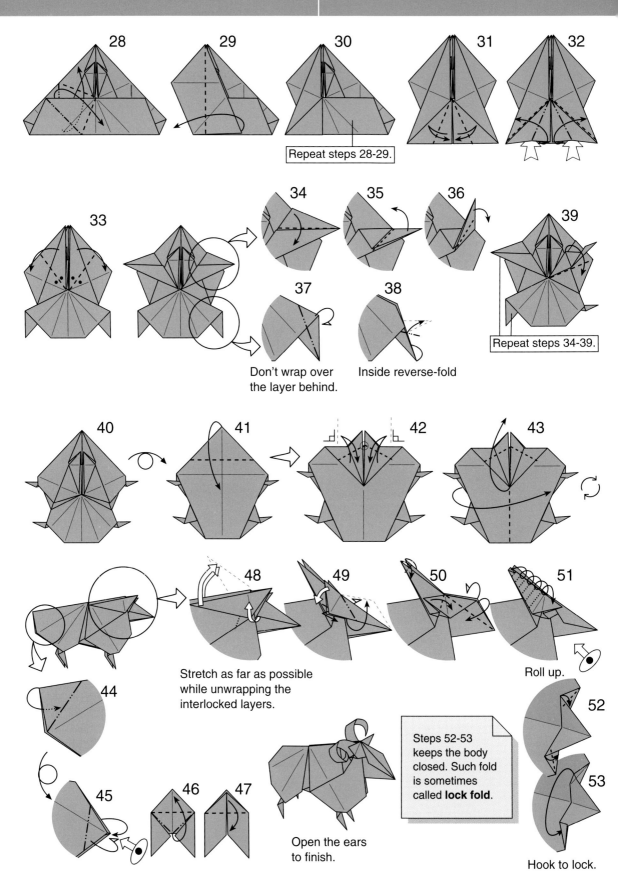

28

29

30

Repeat steps 28-29.

31

32

33

34

35

36

37

38

Don't wrap over
the layer behind.

Inside reverse-fold

39

Repeat steps 34-39.

40

41

42

43

Stretch as far as possible
while unwrapping the
interlocked layers.

48

49

50

51

Roll up.

44

Steps 52-53
keeps the body
closed. Such fold
is sometimes
called **lock fold**.

52

45

46

47

Open the ears
to finish.

53

Hook to lock.

Western Dragon

Theme: Y-pattern

Fold using 6" (15 cm) or preferably larger origami paper.

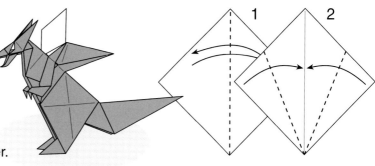

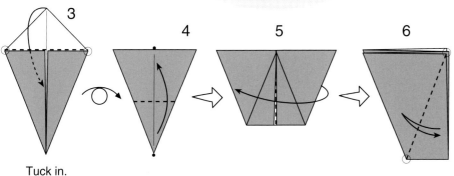

1

2

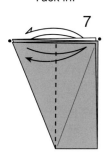

3

Tuck in.

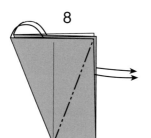

4

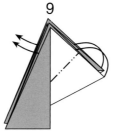

5

6

Pay attention to align the inside reverse folds neatly in steps 8-11.

7

8

Inside reverse-fold

9

Inside reverse-fold

10

Inside reverse-fold

11

Inside reverse-fold

Y pattern

You can see in the crease pattern of *Western Dragon* large and small arrowhead-shaped isosceles triangles (**Y pattern**, shown below). Although it has already appeared repeatedly in *Tree* in **Simple Models** and *Squid* in this chapter, this pattern cannot be seen in any traditional models.

I used to call it "secondary triangle," but in this book I call it "Y pattern."

The discovery of this pattern was one of my breakthroughs in my origami design because, in addition to not being used in traditional models, the pattern has a broad range of applications.

This pattern is a kind of "molecule" as "an area with a set of related creases." But it is not single-value or uniaxial, that is, it cannot be folded so that all the edges align. However, it is still handy as an embedded element of design because the angles are standardized.

This pattern offers a combination of one long flap and two shorter ones.

The crease pattern of *Western Dragon* (mountain and valley folds are not shown).

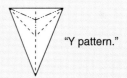

"Y pattern."

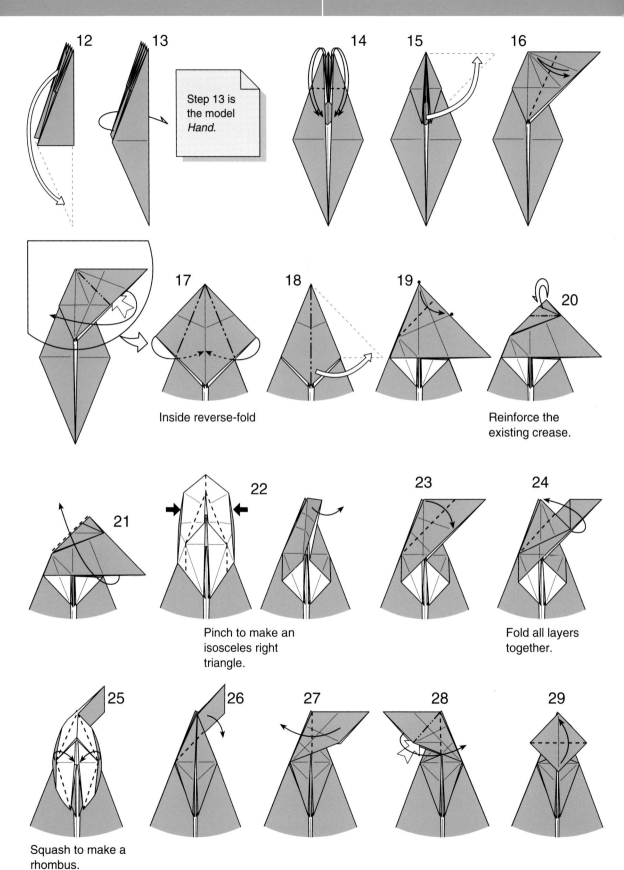

12 13

Step 13 is the model *Hand*.

14 15 16

17 18 19 20

Inside reverse-fold

Reinforce the existing crease.

21 22 23 24

Pinch to make an isosceles right triangle.

Fold all layers together.

25 26 27 28 29

Squash to make a rhombus.

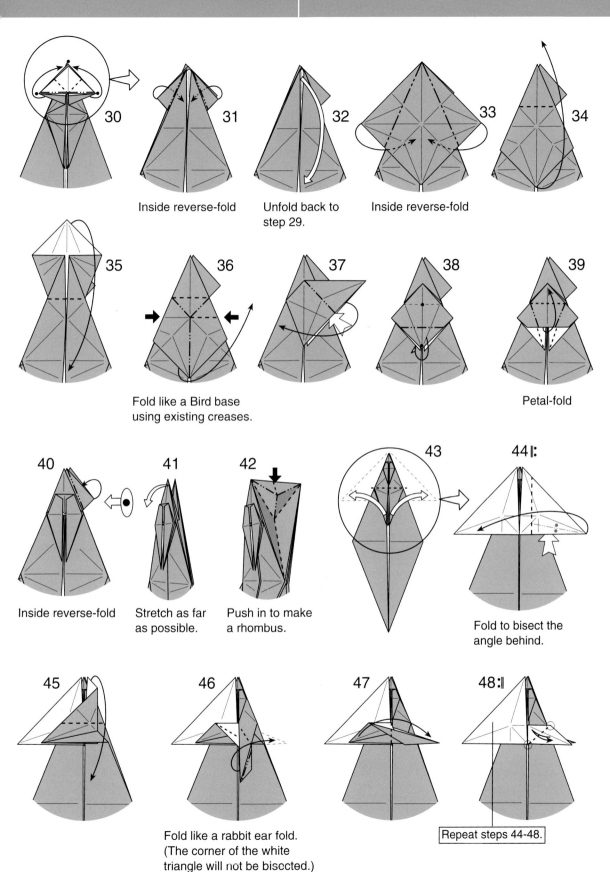

30

31
Inside reverse-fold

32
Unfold back to step 29.

33
Inside reverse-fold

34

35

36
Fold like a Bird base using existing creases.

37

38

39
Petal-fold

40
Inside reverse-fold

41
Stretch as far as possible.

42
Push in to make a rhombus.

43

44 ▯:
Fold to bisect the angle behind.

45

46
Fold like a rabbit ear fold. (The corner of the white triangle will not be bisected.)

47

48 :▯

Repeat steps 44-48.

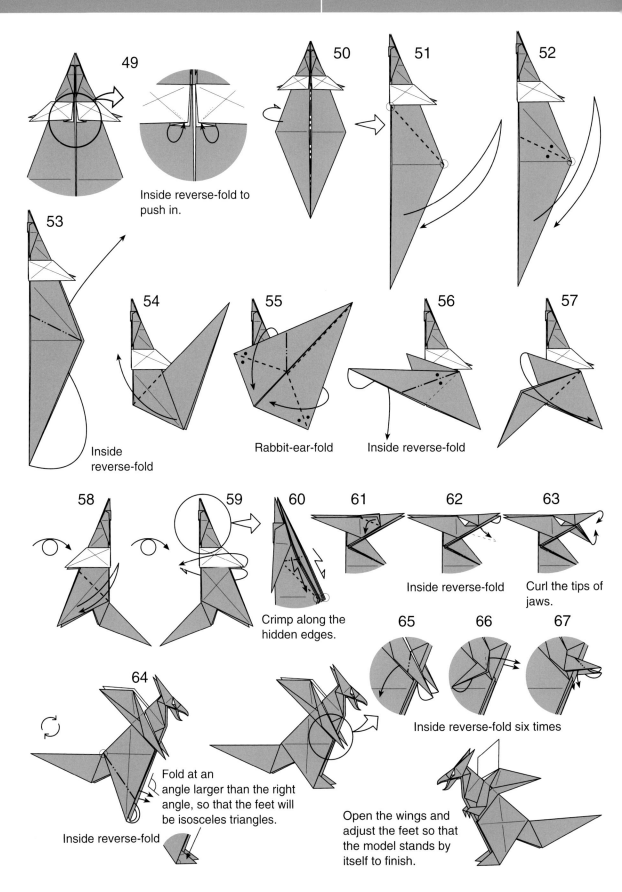

49

Inside reverse-fold to push in.

50

51

52

53

54

55

Rabbit-ear-fold

56

Inside reverse-fold

57

Inside reverse-fold

58

59

60

Crimp along the hidden edges.

61

62

Inside reverse-fold

63

Curl the tips of jaws.

65

66

67

Inside reverse-fold six times

64

Fold at an angle larger than the right angle, so that the feet will be isosceles triangles.

Inside reverse-fold

Open the wings and adjust the feet so that the model stands by itself to finish.

Horse

Theme: Geometric construction

Fold using 6" (15 cm) or
preferably larger origami paper.

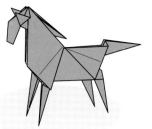

You can draw a line on a
sheet of paper by folding it.
At the same time, you can
use the sheet itself as a
straight-edge and compass,
and beyond.

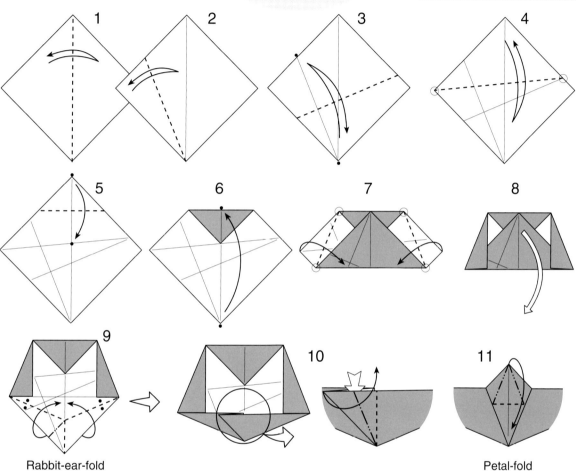

Rabbit-ear-fold

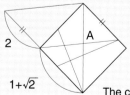

10

11

Petal-fold

Folding the landmark in this model

While the main design aspect of this Horse is its mane, its structure is
the Y pattern at the center with two isosceles right triangles on the sides.
Though it is clear, this structure requires some clever folds to find the
landmark A, which divides the diagonal in $2 : 1+\sqrt{2}$. The picture below
explains the meanings of the construction made in steps 1-4.

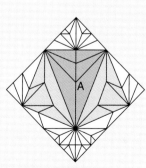

2

A

$1+\sqrt{2}$

We extend the side to obtain the
desired ratio, and transfer that
ratio onto the diagonal by folding
the parallel line. This method can
be applied in many cases.

The construction made in step 1-4

The crease pattern of *Horse* (mountain
and valley folds are not shown;
underlying triangles are shown in gray).

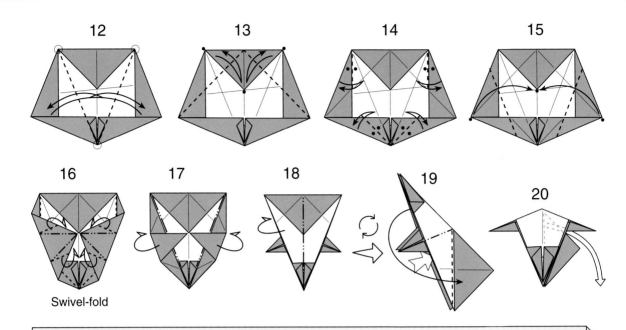

Swivel-fold

Constructions in origami

We have already seen some constructions in this book, such as the trisection of a side with Haga theorem in *Conch*, dividing a side into five in *Gift Box*, and folding the golden ratio in *Connected Cranes: Kotobuki*. Because folding flat is equal to drawing a straight line, it is natural to regard origami as a tool for geometric constructions.

Humiaki Huzita formulated six folds, each of which draws one straight line that has definite landmarks, and Jacques Justin added the seventh. Huzita called them axioms, but they are not axioms in the mathematical sense. They are rather "origami procedure that draws one straight line."

1. Fold a point onto another point.
2. Fold a line onto another line.
3. Fold along the line connecting two points.
4. Fold along the line that passes through a point and is perpendicular to a line.
5. Fold along the line that passes through a point and places another point onto a line.
6. Fold a point onto a line and another point onto another line.
7. Fold along the line that places a point onto a line and is perpendicular to another line.

The combination of folds 1 through 5 is equivalent to solving quadratic equations, which in turn is equivalent to the constructions with a straight-edge and compass. The construction in this *Horse* and other constructions like making a pentagon are possible with these folds. A typical example of fold 4 is step 4 of *Tree*, and that of fold 5 is step 3 of *Penguin*, which comes later in this book.

By adding fold 6, some constructions that are impossible with a straight-edge and compass become possible, since the fold is equivalent to solving cubic equations. Fold 6 is not unnatural. In fact, fold 3, which corresponds to drawing a line with a straight-edge, is sometimes more difficult than fold 6 unless points are placed on the edges.

Hisashi Abe emphasized these when he solved two of three **Classical Greek Problems**, **angle trisection** and **doubling the cube**, using fold 6.

Note that these two problems cannot be solved with finite procedures of a straight-edge and compass. In the 19th century, Pierre Wantzel proved this by relating geometric constructions to the order of equations. It is also known that these constructions are possible if we use special tools. That is, origami is just one of such tools that is different from a straight-edge and compass. The other problem, **squaring a circle**, is also proved to be impossible because it involves the circular constant, which makes this problem more difficult.

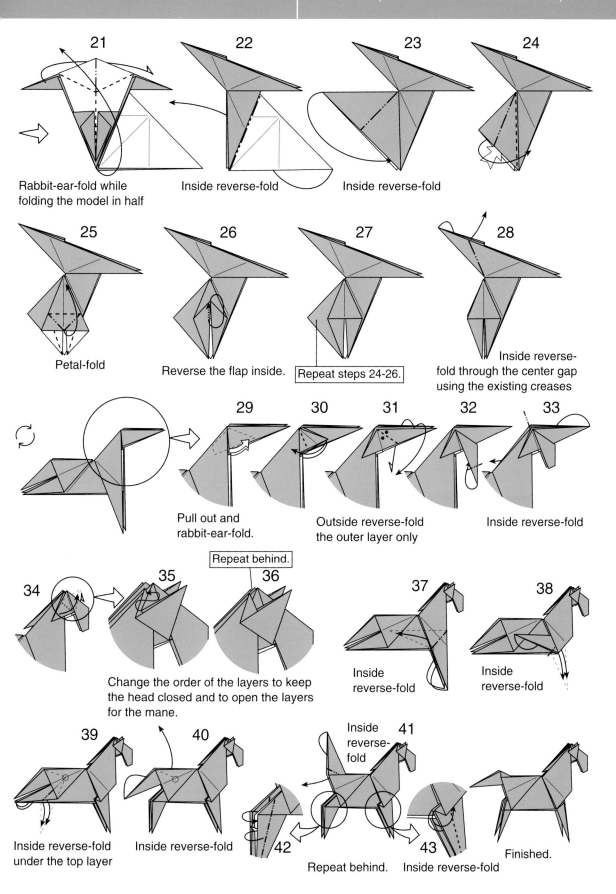

21 Rabbit-ear-fold while folding the model in half

22 Inside reverse-fold

23 Inside reverse-fold

24

25 Petal-fold

26 Reverse the flap inside.

27 Repeat steps 24-26.

28 Inside reverse-fold through the center gap using the existing creases

29 Pull out and rabbit-ear-fold.

30 Outside reverse-fold the outer layer only

31

32

33 Inside reverse-fold

34

35

Repeat behind.

36 Change the order of the layers to keep the head closed and to open the layers for the mane.

37 Inside reverse-fold

38 Inside reverse-fold

39 Inside reverse-fold under the top layer

40 Inside reverse-fold

41 Inside reverse-fold

42 Repeat behind.

43 Inside reverse-fold

Finished.

Triceratops

Theme: Open-back, Open-belly

Fold using 6" (15 cm) or
preferably larger origami paper.

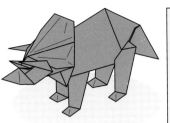

This model, like Horse, requires some construction to find the landmark.

Steps 1-3 indicates the ratio of $\sqrt{2} : 1+\sqrt{2}$.

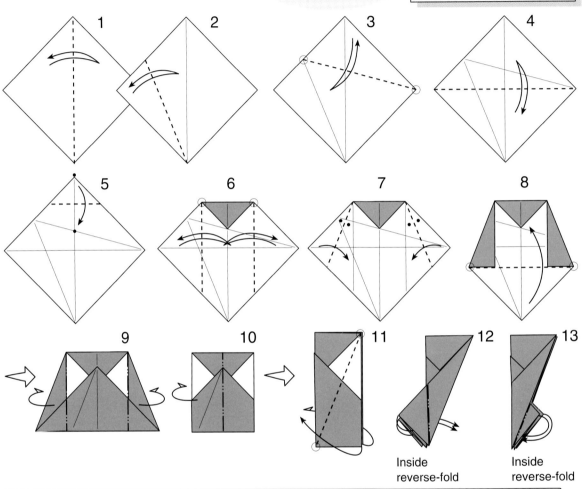

1 2 3 4

5 6 7 8

9 10 11 12 13

Inside reverse-fold

Inside reverse-fold

Open-back and open-belly

The design of origami animals can be classified by their cross sections, as shown below. Open-back design should be avoided when we want to emphasize the broad back of an animal. A Triceratops is one of such animals. I once designed a triceratops, with the almost same crease pattern as this model, using "open-back #2" design. But I was not satisfied for that reason, and modified the model by reversing upside down. Then I was able to change the crease pattern to a nice "open-belly" design.

 Open-back #1   Open-belly   Open-back #2   Closed

Such reverse method does not always work well. But reversing an existing design upside down or front-side back often results in a different "mitate." For example, if you reverse the head and tail of *Three-headed Crane*, you may see it as a phoenix, if not a crane.

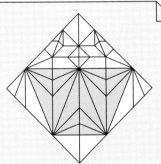

The crease pattern of *Triceratops* (mountain and valley folds are not shown; "Y patterns" are shown in gray).

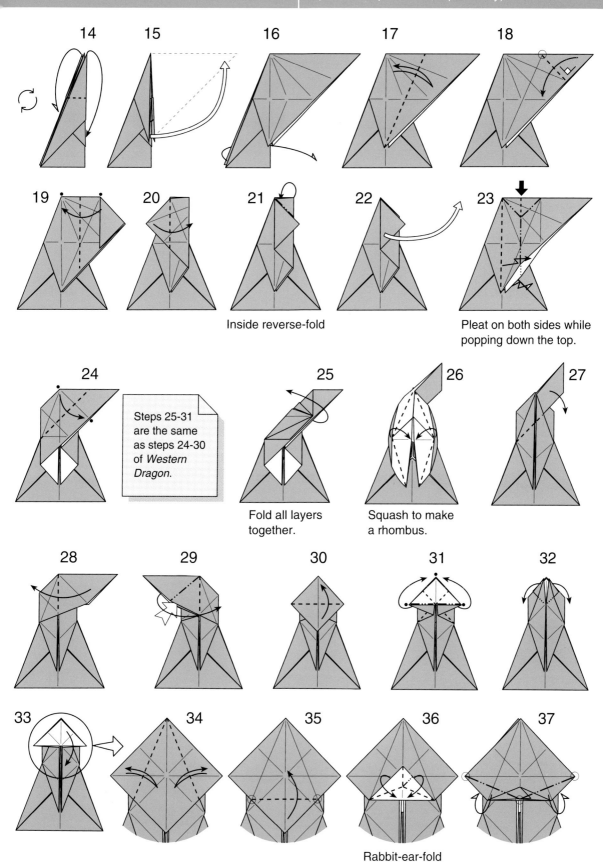

14 15 16 17 18

19 20 21 22 23

Inside reverse-fold

Pleat on both sides while
popping down the top.

24

Steps 25-31
are the same
as steps 24-30
of *Western
Dragon*.

25 26 27

Fold all layers
together.

Squash to make
a rhombus.

28 29 30 31 32

33 34 35 36 37

Rabbit-ear-fold

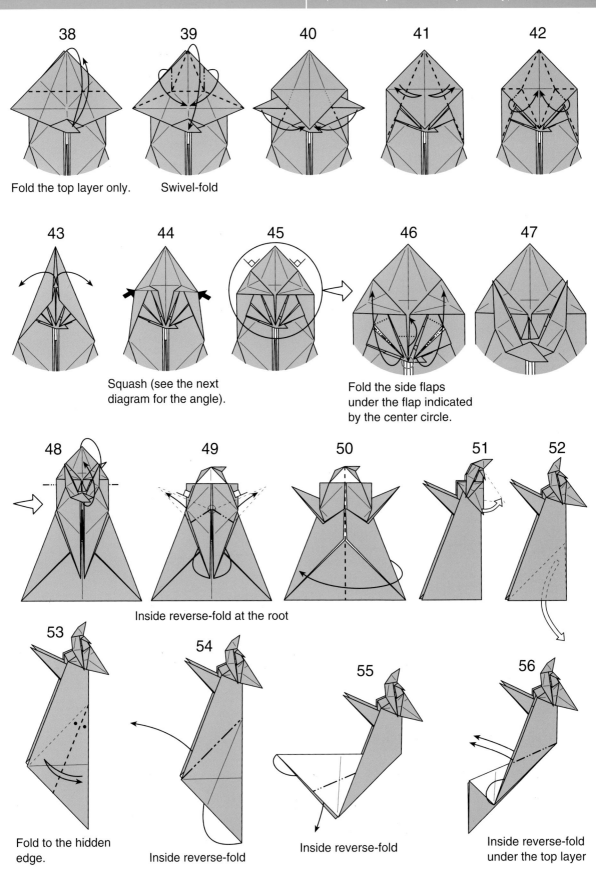

38 Fold the top layer only.

39 Swivel-fold

40

41

42

43

44 Squash (see the next diagram for the angle).

45

46 Fold the side flaps under the flap indicated by the center circle.

47

48

49 Inside reverse-fold at the root

50

51

52

53 Fold to the hidden edge.

54 Inside reverse-fold

55 Inside reverse-fold

56 Inside reverse-fold under the top layer

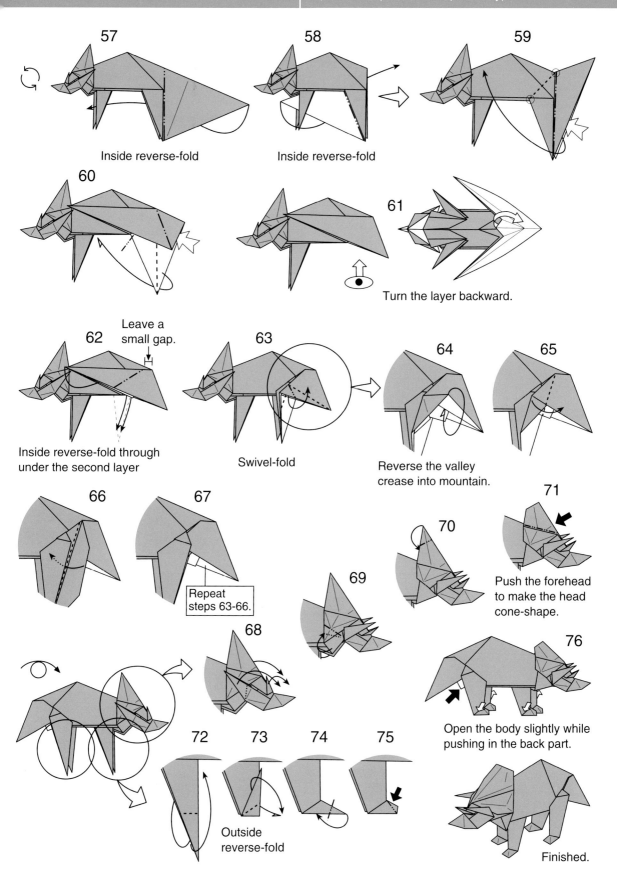

57 Inside reverse-fold

58 Inside reverse-fold

59

60

61 Turn the layer backward.

62 Leave a small gap.
Inside reverse-fold through under the second layer

63 Swivel-fold

64 Reverse the valley crease into mountain.

65

66

67 Repeat steps 63-66.

68

69

70

71 Push the forehead to make the head cone-shape.

72

73 Outside reverse-fold

74

75

76 Open the body slightly while pushing in the back part.

Finished.

Rabbit

Theme: Solid body

Fold using 6" (15 cm) origami paper.

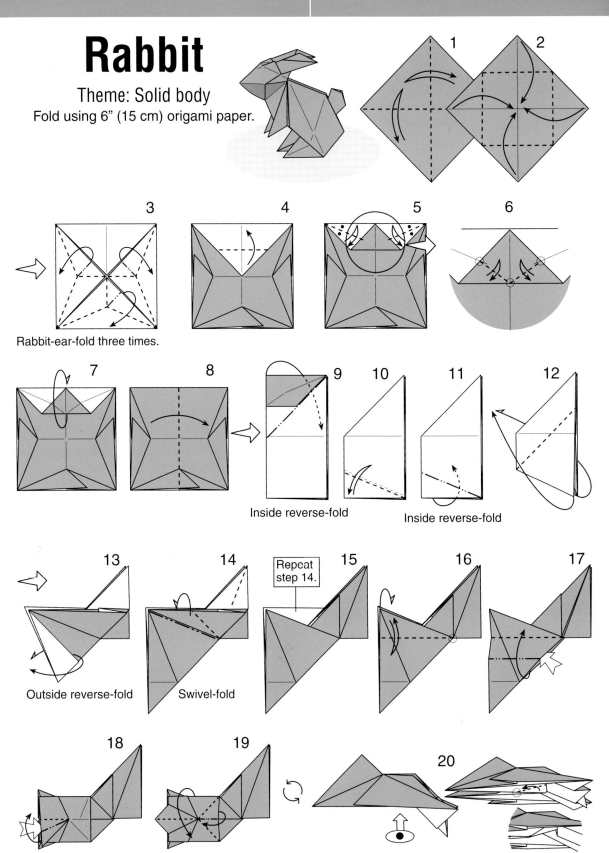

3 — Rabbit-ear-fold three times.

9 — Inside reverse-fold

11 — Inside reverse-fold

13 — Outside reverse-fold

14 — Swivel-fold

Repeat step 14.

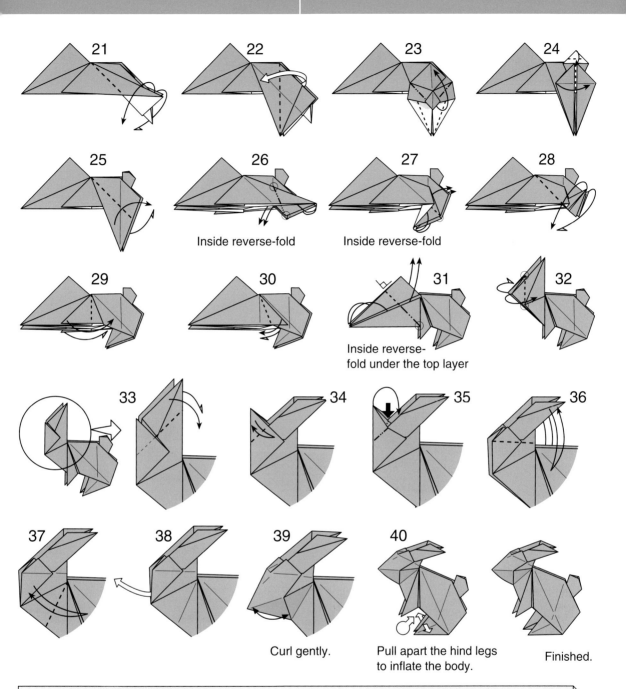

Inside reverse-fold

Inside reverse-fold

Inside reverse-fold under the top layer

Curl gently.

Pull apart the hind legs to inflate the body.

Finished.

Three-dimensional design

I have explained origami design from the viewpoint of branches. But the shape of the model's face is also important. For example, the Bird base is characterized not only by its four long flaps but also by the shape of them.

Speaking of faces, origami models can be seen as a kind of polyhedra, though most of them are flat. Even when the finished model is three-dimensional,

the underlying design is often flat, and the model is just made three-dimensional with shaping (see *Dolphin*).

There are, however, models designed to be three-dimensional. Among already-introduced models, *Squid* is a typical example. And this *Rabbit* makes use of such design in a simple way in its oval head. Compare it with the body, which is made three-dimensional with shaping.

Tiger Mask

Theme: Polyhedron

Fold using 6" (15 cm) origami paper.

1

2

3

4

5

6

Don't crease here.

7

Unwrap.

8

Valley-fold here.

Fold like a Bird base.

9

10

11

Polyhedral design

In designing a three-dimensional model as in a non-flat polyhedron, the important thing is to determine how to place the faces that will appear on the surface of the model.

The composition of faces for Tiger Mask is shown on the right. It resembles more to paper-craft development diagrams than crease patterns. But this is not a paper-craft model because it is folded without cuts. We do not cut off the white areas.

There is a basic rule in placing faces. If the corner is either convex or concave, then faces can touch each other at the corner.

On the other hand, if the corner is a saddle point, in other words, the faces form a saddle surface (shown on the right) around it, then the faces must be placed separately at appropriate distances. Some areas must be pleated and hidden, because the angle around the corner is larger than 360°. In this model, there are two saddle points at each side of the nose.

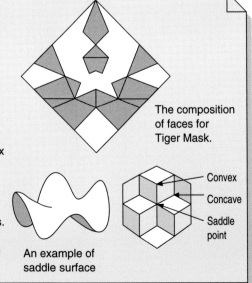

The composition of faces for Tiger Mask.

An example of saddle surface

Convex
Concave
Saddle point

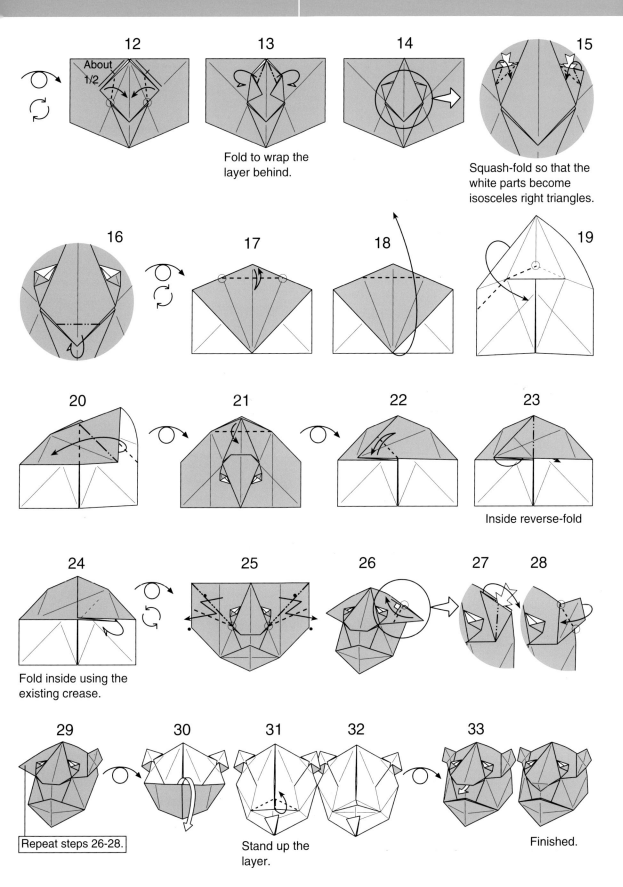

12 About 1/2

13 Fold to wrap the layer behind.

14

15 Squash-fold so that the white parts become isosceles right triangles.

16

17

18

19

20

21

22

23 Inside reverse-fold

24 Fold inside using the existing crease.

25

26

27

28

29 Repeat steps 26-28.

30

31 Stand up the layer.

32

33 Finished.

Devil Mask

Theme: Variation

Fold using 6" (15 cm) origami paper.

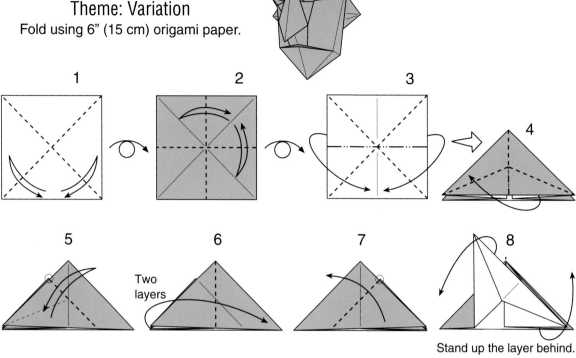

1

2

3

4

5

6

Two layers

7

8

Stand up the layer behind.

9

Squash symmetrically.

10

11

Fold like a Bird base.

12

13

14

15

16

Joy of making variations

I wanted to apply the design of *Tiger Mask* to a human face, instead of an animal. But the forehead is too small for a human (well, the devil, in this case), so I modified the composition by changing the axis of symmetry, as in *Squid*. You can multiply the number of variations of one model in similar ways. This is part of the joys of origami design.

Tiger Mask

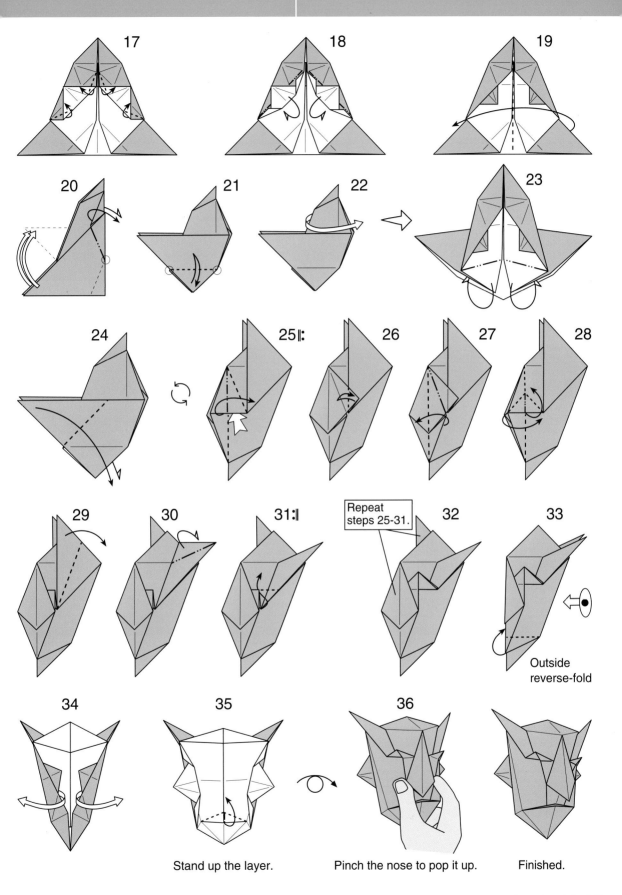

17

18

19

20

21

22

23

24

25 ‖:

26

27

28

29

30

31 :‖

Repeat steps 25-31.

32

33

Outside reverse-fold

34

35

36

Stand up the layer.

Pinch the nose to pop it up.

Finished.

Penguin

Theme: 15 degrees; Cone

Fold using 6" (15 cm) origami paper.

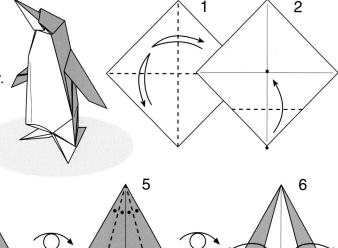

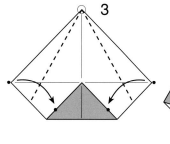
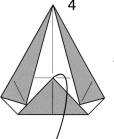
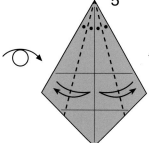
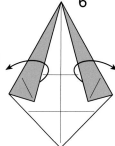

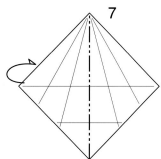
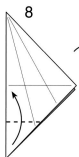
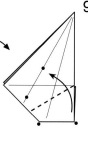
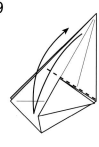
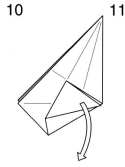

Using the 15° angle

The unit of angle in this model is not 22.5°, or a fourth of the right angle, but 15°, or a sixth of the right angle. The 15° angle is compatible with the square. You will notice that many points and lines meet each other in the sequence.

When we standardize the angle, we must define a unit angle. According to my experience, 15° and 22.5° are the most suitable to design, 30° is less suitable, and 18° and other degrees are difficult to use. When the unit is 15°, there are twelve types of triangle faces, which is much more than compared to the five when the unit is 22.5° (see *Wild Boar*). Among the twelve triangles shown on the right, three in the top row are basic.

The unit angle can also be 45°. That is equal to simple box-pleating (see *Snake*). I said "simple" because of the following reasons.

What is standardized in box-pleating structure is the position of corners, rather than the angle, of creases. Using "advanced" box-pleating, we can make an ordered structure that is not based on any division of 360°.

Triangles based on 15° angle units

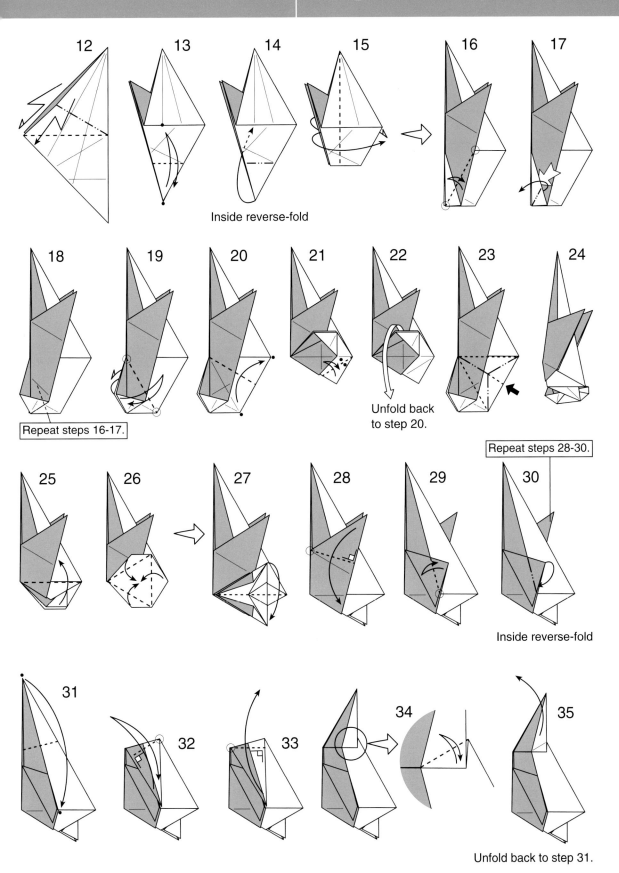

Inside reverse-fold

Repeat steps 16-17.

Unfold back to step 20.

Repeat steps 28-30.

Inside reverse-fold

Unfold back to step 31.

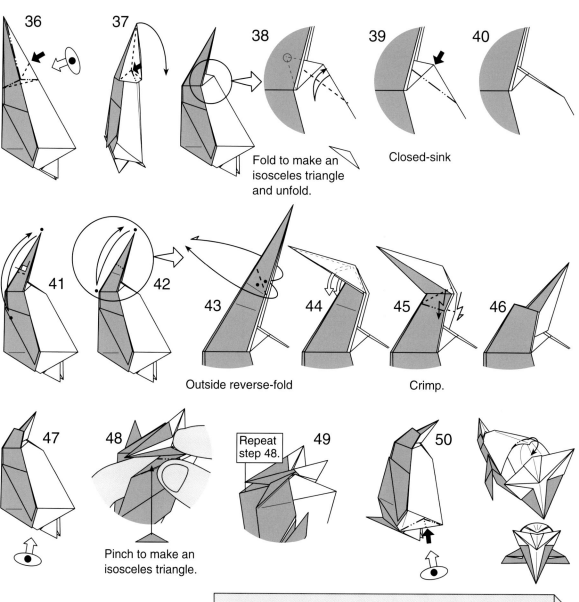

38 Fold to make an isosceles triangle and unfold.

39 Closed-sink

Outside reverse-fold

Crimp.

48 Pinch to make an isosceles triangle.

49 Repeat step 48.

51

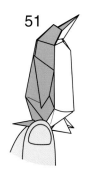

Reinforce the creases made in steps 48 and 49 to keep the back closed.

Finished.

Curved surfaces that can be made from flat surfaces.
Although any curved surface, when divided into tiny areas, can be approximated from a plane, only three types of curved surface are developable, in other words, can be developed onto a plane. They are the conical, cylindrical, and tangent surfaces. The basic idea of *Penguin* is, besides using 15° angle unit, making a three-dimensional body with a conical surface instead of a polyhedron that is a combination of planes. The earlier version of this model was closer to the cone.

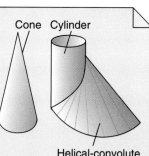

Cone Cylinder

Helical-convolute surface

Examples of conical, cylindrical, and tangent surfaces: a cone, a cylinder, and a helical-convolute surface.

Frog

Theme: Approximation

Fold using 6" (15 cm) origami paper.

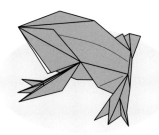

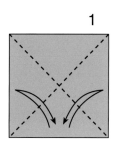

1

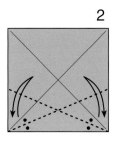

2

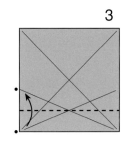

3

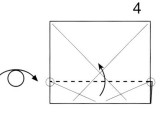

4

5

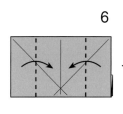

6

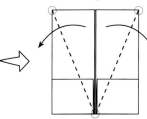

7

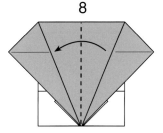

8

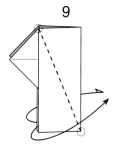

9

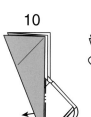

10

11

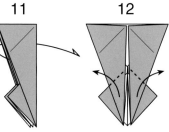

12

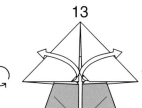

13

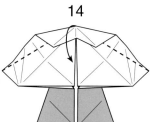

14

Inside reverse-fold

Approximation

If you calculate assuming that the angles of creases are multiples of 22.5°, then the crease pattern of this *Frog* does not fit in a square, as shown on the right. The ratio of the height to the width is about 1.017...

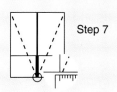

Step 7

Theoretically, there is a gap of about 1/16".

That means, when folded using 6" (15 cm) paper, there is a gap of about 1/16" (1 mm) at step 7. But in practice, you do not have to bother about it. For some models, folding precisely is essential because errors will be magnified through the sequence. But for other models like this, errors will be absorbed in paper. That is one of the differences between real-world origami and pure geometry, where lines have no width and surfaces have no thickness.

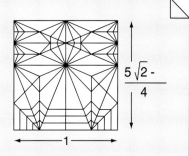

$$\frac{5\sqrt{2} - }{4}$$

1

The crease pattern of *Frog* (mountain and valley folds are not shown).

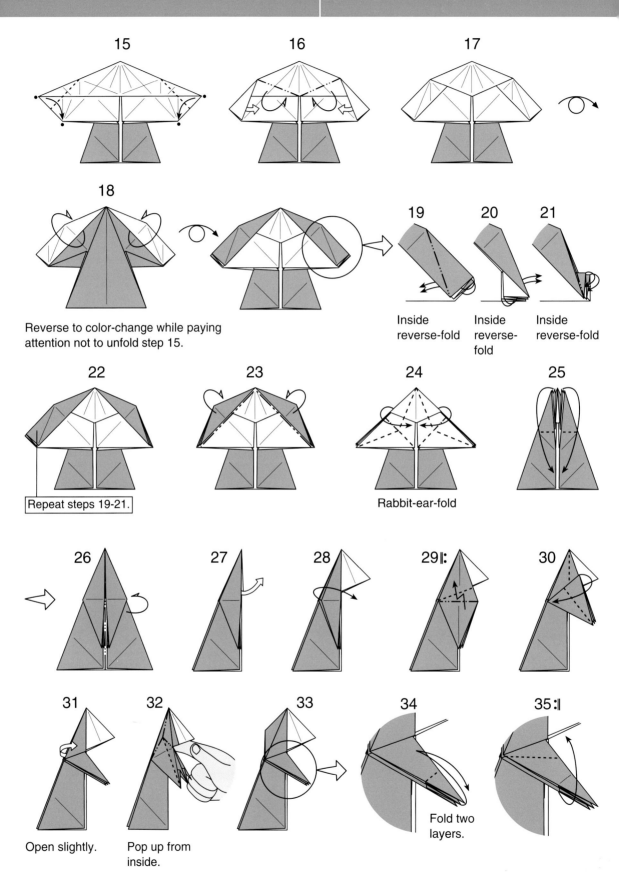

15 **16** **17**

18

Reverse to color-change while paying attention not to unfold step 15.

19 **20** **21**

Inside reverse-fold

Inside reverse-fold

Inside reverse-fold

22 **23** **24** **25**

Repeat steps 19-21.

Rabbit-ear-fold

26 **27** **28** **29** **30**

31 **32** **33** **34** **35**

Open slightly.

Pop up from inside.

Fold two layers.

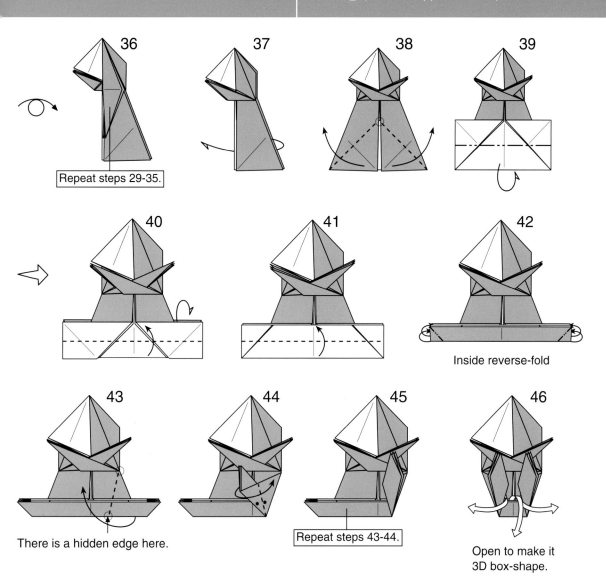

Repeat steps 29-35.

Inside reverse-fold

There is a hidden edge here.

Repeat steps 43-44.

Open to make it 3D box-shape.

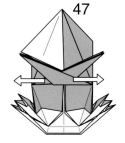

Pull apart as far as possible.

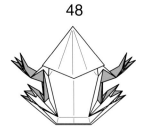

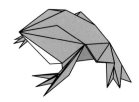

Adjust the model so that it stands on its toes to finish.

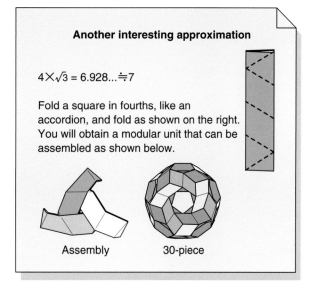

Another interesting approximation

$4 \times \sqrt{3} = 6.928... \fallingdotseq 7$

Fold a square in fourths, like an accordion, and fold as shown on the right. You will obtain a modular unit that can be assembled as shown below.

Assembly   30-piece

Pyramid

Theme: Infinite folding

Fold using 6" (15 cm) or
preferably larger origami paper.

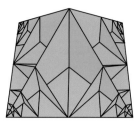

Although the sequence is
diagrammed in 33 steps, you
can, in theory, repeat the
steps as many times as you
want.

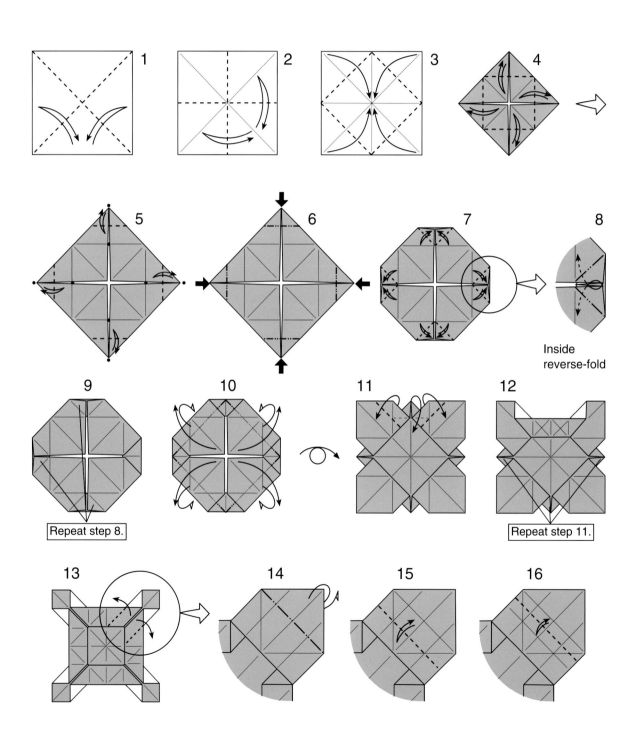

Inside
reverse-fold

Repeat step 8.

Repeat step 11.

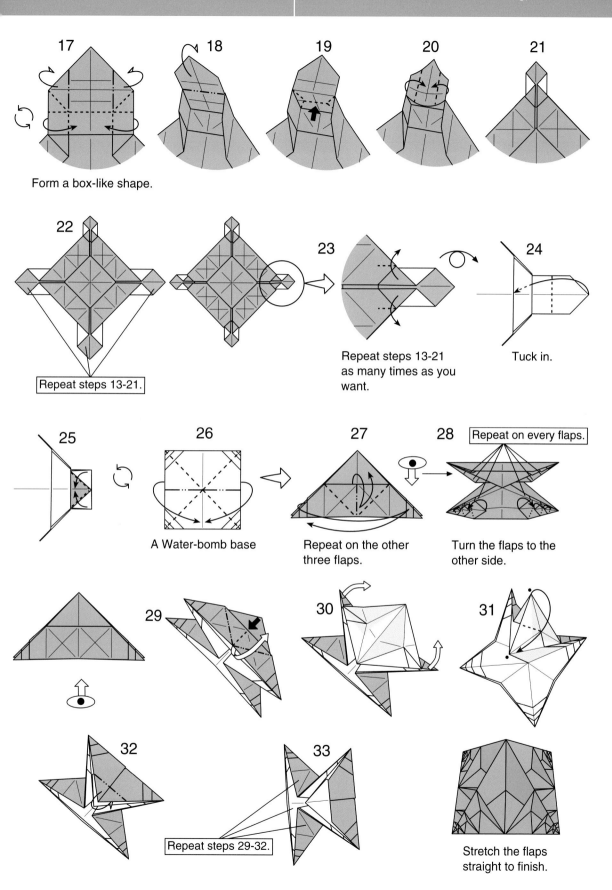

17 Form a box-like shape.

18

19

20

21

22 Repeat steps 13-21.

23 Repeat steps 13-21 as many times as you want.

24 Tuck in.

25

26 A Water-bomb base

27 Repeat on the other three flaps.

28 Repeat on every flaps. Turn the flaps to the other side.

29

30

31

32

33 Repeat steps 29-32.

Stretch the flaps straight to finish.

Folding infinitely

This model Pyramid consists of four similar patterns, each one consisted by smaller and smaller triangular plates converging to one point.

Though it may look like branches of a tree, no branch has a sub-branch, unlike *Turkey* that is introduced later.

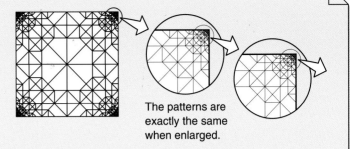

The patterns are exactly the same when enlarged.

Ushio Ikegami extended this model and achieved a crease pattern that branches both infinitely and recursively. Its structure is highly complex but very interesting.

Folding a mathematically-correct pyramid

In the real pyramids in Giza, the ratio of the height to the base is said to be 1 : 1.618... or the golden ratio. On the other hand, the ratio in this model, where the sides are equilateral triangles, is 1.414... or $\sqrt{2}$, which is slightly different from "true pyramid."

Interestingly, if the ratio of the base to the height in a square pyramid is the golden ratio, the ratio in the side is 2 : 1.589..., which is nearly equal to the golden ratio.

I found an article "Folding true pyramids" in my own old design notes, where I assumed that the ratio of the base to the height in the side should be 2 to the golden ratio. Some sketches from the article are shown below.

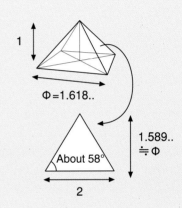

$\Phi = 1.618..$

$1.589.. \fallingdotseq \Phi$

About 58°

B A

B

A

Two types of pyramid without the bottom

A pyramid with the bottom, folded from a rotated Water-bomb base

If folded from a regular Water-bomb base, the vertex angle of each triangle will be greater than 60°, and there will be folded edges on the sides. But the difference can be ignored in practice.

This concludes Intermediate Models.

The next chapter is Complex Models. The models are difficult to fold just because they have detailed folds and many steps. That does not mean simpler models have lower qualities.

As I said at the end of Simple Models, there is no definitive standard for complexity levels in origami. But it is true that the models in Complex Models have a lot more detailed folds. Still, those who have completed the models in this chapter should be ready to fold them without difficulty.

Chick

Theme: Deltahedron
This model is based on one type of deltahedron, a polyhedron whose faces are equilateral triangles, called triangular dipyramid.

Peacock

Theme: Miura-ori; Tessellation
The pattern for the tail of this model is the same as Miura-ori, a famous result of engineering of origami.

Turkey

Theme: Self-similar
The creases in this model repeat the same pattern in a nesting structure, which relates to fractal geometry.

Chapter 5
Complex Models

"Origami is the multi-dimensional Eulerian path."
M. J.

Tyrannosaurus

Theme: Realism
One of the main incentives for origami design is the challenge to realistic illustration.

Eastern Dragon

Theme: Grafting
Explains grafting, or adding new elements to an existing model, using the design of claws of this model as a typical example.

Samurai Helmet Beetle

Theme: No glue, no cuts
Examines the "no glue" rule, one of the basic rules often applied to origami.

Devil

Theme: Taming the devil
Introduces my first-ever published and representative model to conclude this book.

Chick

Theme: Deltahedron
Fold using 6" (15 cm) origami paper.

This design came from an image of an egg with legs and a head.

To realize the oval shape, I used one type of deltahedron called triangular dipyramid as its base.

Regular polyhedron and deltahedron
A regular polyhedron is a polyhedron whose faces are congruent regular polygons and whose corners are inscribed in a sphere. There are only five types of regular polyhedron, the tetrahedron, the hexahedron (or the cube), the octahedron, the dodecahedron, and the icosahedron.
Among them, the tetrahedron, the octahedron, and the icosahedron have equilateral triangle faces. There are several other convex polyhedra (polyhedra that include in its volume any line connecting two points on its surface) whose faces are equilateral triangles. Such a polyhedron is called deltahedron. There are eight types, including three types of regular polyhedron. The number of faces is 4, 6, 8, 10, 12, 14, 16, or 20. It is interesting that there is not a deltahedron that has 18 faces.

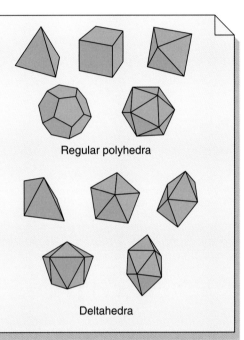

Regular polyhedra

Understanding the shapes of these polyhedra and their truncated families (for example, a cuboctahedron is shown on the left) will add to some "aha effect" during the assembly of modular origami models.

Deltahedra

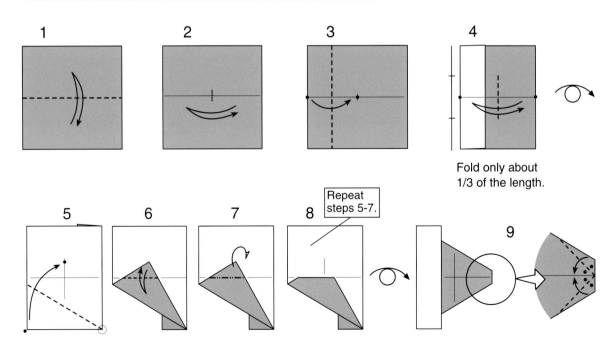

Fold only about 1/3 of the length.

Repeat steps 5-7.

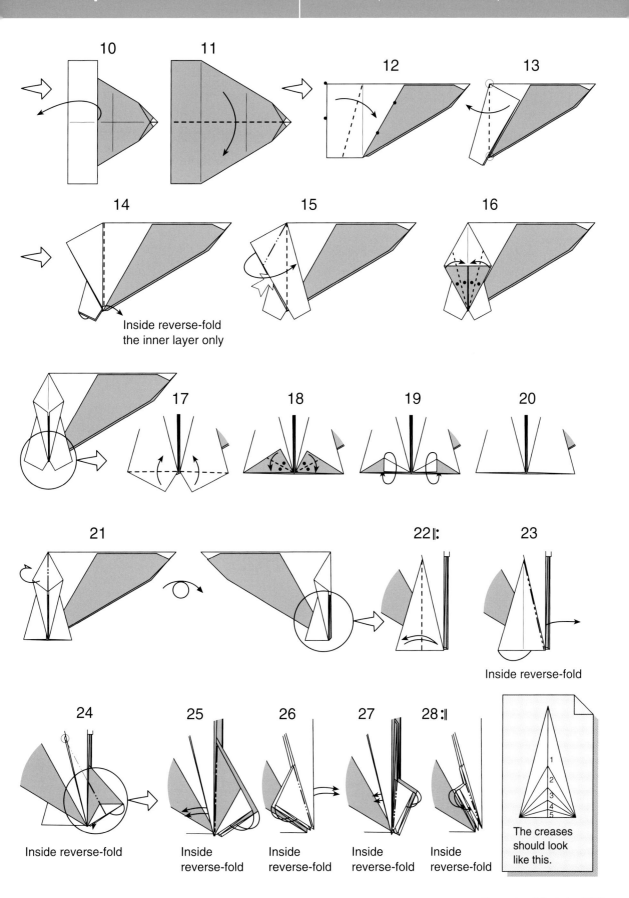

10

11

12

13

14

Inside reverse-fold
the inner layer only

15

16

17

18

19

20

21

22 ‖:

23

Inside reverse-fold

24

Inside reverse-fold

25

Inside
reverse-fold

26

Inside
reverse-fold

27

Inside
reverse-fold

28 :‖

Inside
reverse-fold

The creases
should look
like this.

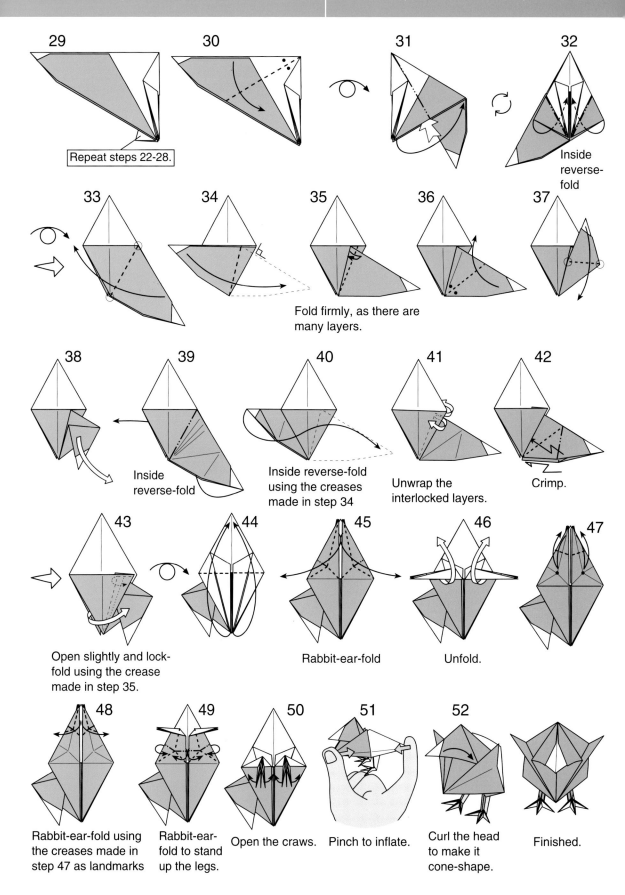

29

Repeat steps 22-28.

30

31

32 Inside reverse-fold

33

34

35 Fold firmly, as there are many layers.

36

37

38

39 Inside reverse-fold

40 Inside reverse-fold using the creases made in step 34

41 Unwrap the interlocked layers.

42 Crimp.

43 Open slightly and lock-fold using the crease made in step 35.

44

45 Rabbit-ear-fold

46 Unfold.

47

48 Rabbit-ear-fold using the creases made in step 47 as landmarks

49 Rabbit-ear-fold to stand up the legs.

50 Open the craws.

51 Pinch to inflate.

52 Curl the head to make it cone-shape.

Finished.

Peacock

Theme: Miura-ori; Tessellation

Fold using 6" (15 cm) or
preferably larger origami paper.

> I present you two types of
> this model. First fold *Peacock
> 1*, with fewer pleats, as a
> warm-up, then proceed to
> *Peacock 2*, which is a more
> advanced model with twice as
> many pleats.

Peacock 1

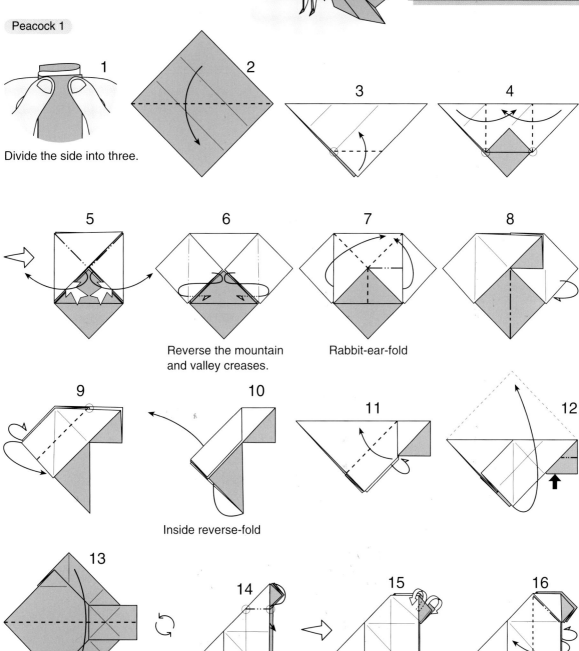

1

Divide the side into three.

2

3

4

5

6

Reverse the mountain
and valley creases.

7

Rabbit-ear-fold

8

9

10

Inside reverse-fold

11

12

13

14

Inside reverse-fold

15

Reverse like an outside
reverse fold.

16

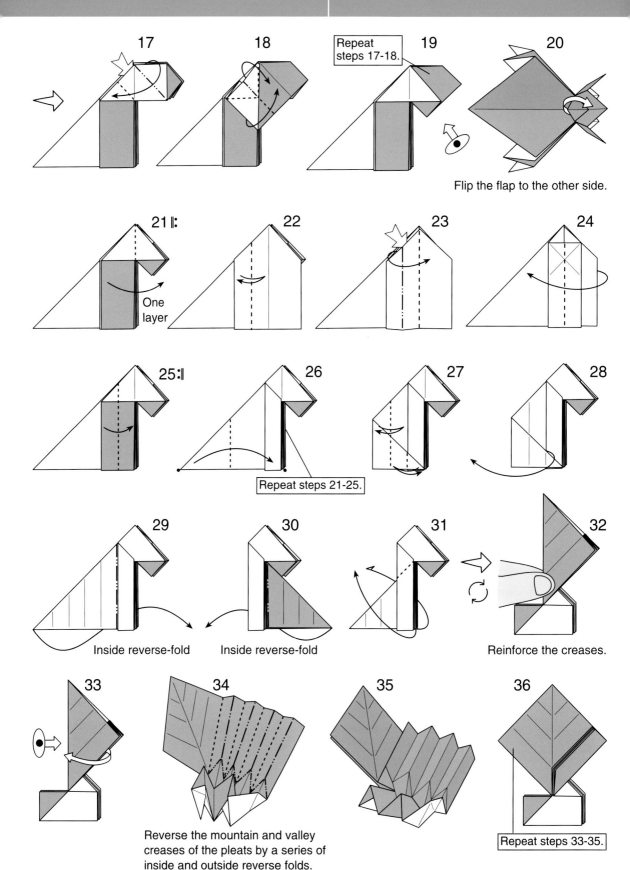

17

18

19
Repeat steps 17-18.

20
Flip the flap to the other side.

21
One layer

22

23

24

25

26
Repeat steps 21-25.

27

28

29
Inside reverse-fold

30
Inside reverse-fold

31

32
Reinforce the creases.

33

34
Reverse the mountain and valley creases of the pleats by a series of inside and outside reverse folds.

35

36
Repeat steps 33-35.

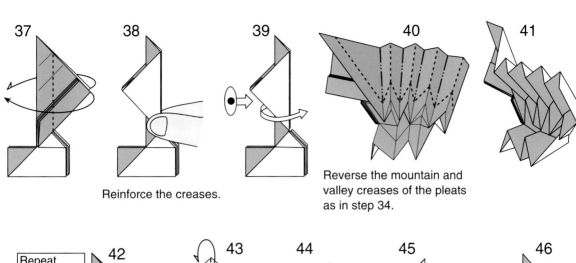

37

38

Reinforce the creases.

39

40

Reverse the mountain and valley creases of the pleats as in step 34.

41

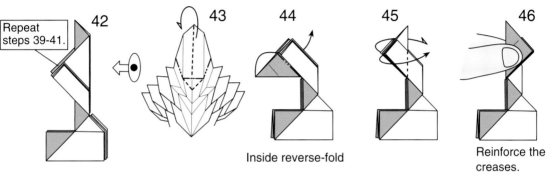

Repeat steps 39-41.

42

43

44

45

46

Inside reverse-fold

Reinforce the creases.

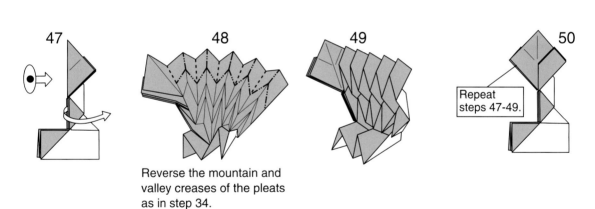

47

48

Reverse the mountain and valley creases of the pleats as in step 34.

49

50

Repeat steps 47-49.

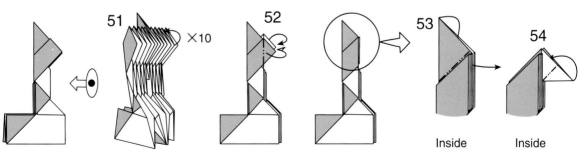

51

×10

Inside reverse-fold ten times

52

53

54

Inside reverse-fold

Inside reverse-fold

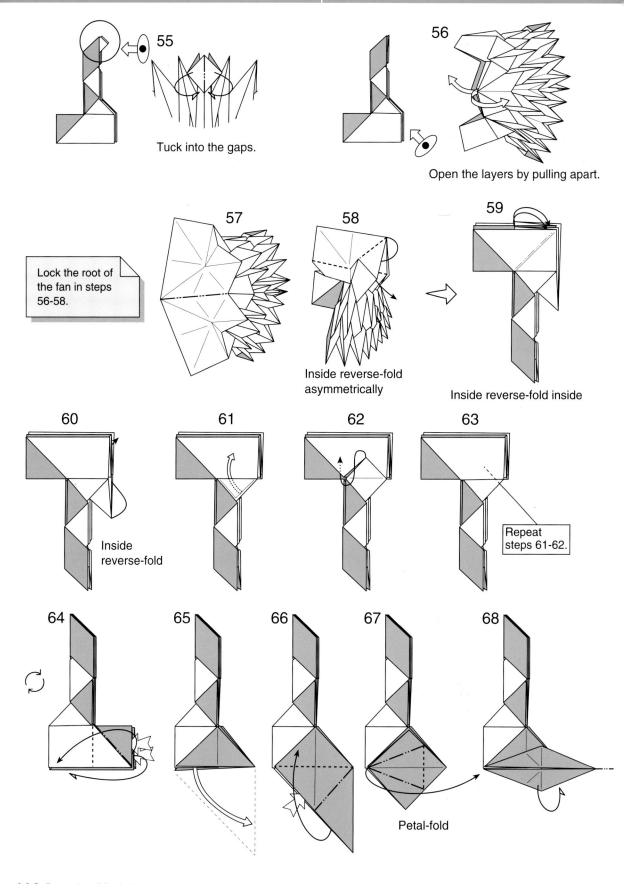

55 Tuck into the gaps.

56 Open the layers by pulling apart.

Lock the root of the fan in steps 56-58.

57

58 Inside reverse-fold asymmetrically

59 Inside reverse-fold inside

60 Inside reverse-fold

61

62

63 Repeat steps 61-62.

64

65

66

67 Petal-fold

68

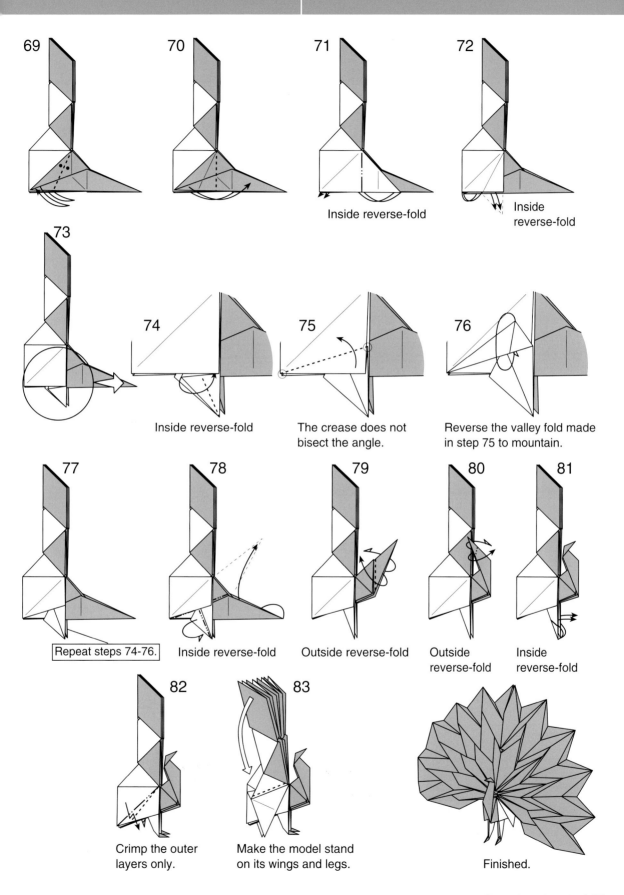

69

70

71

Inside reverse-fold

72

Inside reverse-fold

73

74

Inside reverse-fold

75

The crease does not bisect the angle.

76

Reverse the valley fold made in step 75 to mountain.

77

Repeat steps 74-76.

78

Inside reverse-fold

79

Outside reverse-fold

80

Outside reverse-fold

81

Inside reverse-fold

82

Crimp the outer layers only.

83

Make the model stand on its wings and legs.

Finished.

Peacock 2

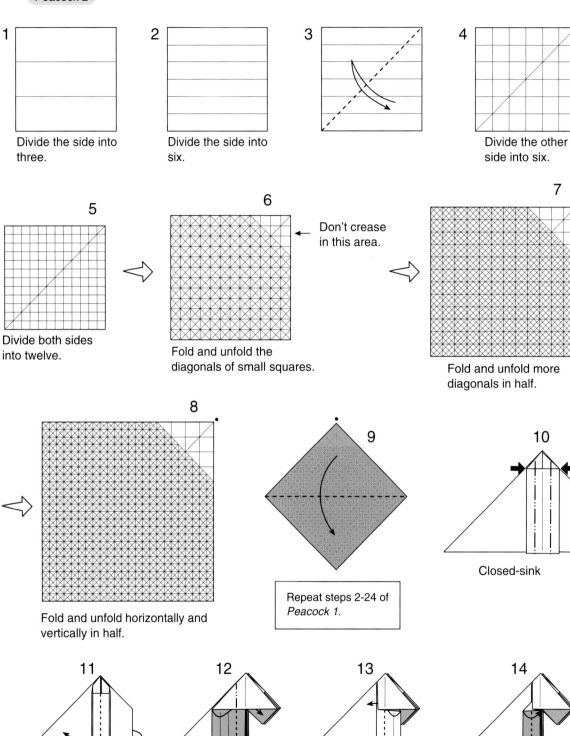

1 Divide the side into three.

2 Divide the side into six.

3

4 Divide the other side into six.

5 Divide both sides into twelve.

6 Fold and unfold the diagonals of small squares.

Don't crease in this area.

7 Fold and unfold more diagonals in half.

8 Fold and unfold horizontally and vertically in half.

9 Repeat steps 2-24 of *Peacock 1*.

10 Closed-sink

11

12 Inside reverse-fold

13 Inside reverse-fold

14 Inside reverse-fold

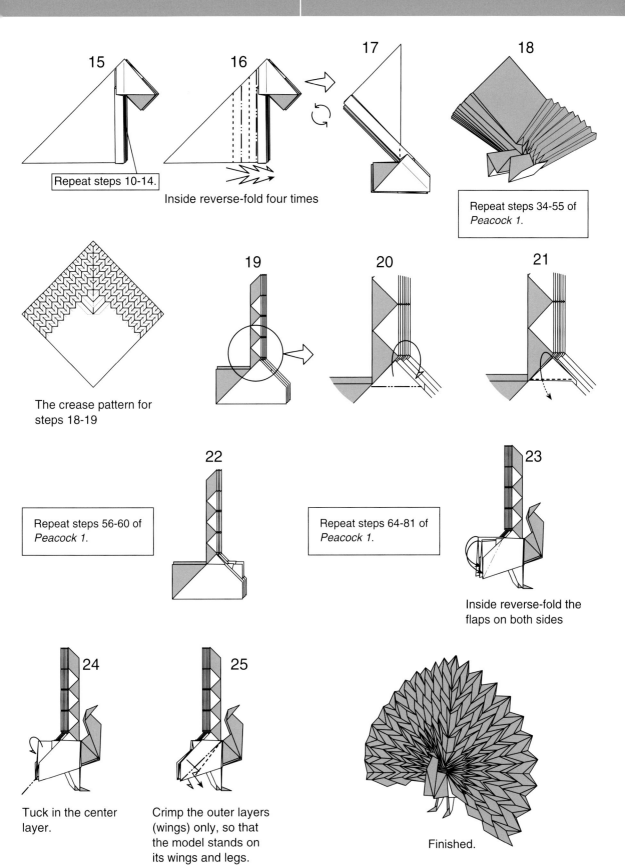

15

Repeat steps 10-14.

16

Inside reverse-fold four times

17

18

Repeat steps 34-55 of *Peacock 1*.

The crease pattern for steps 18-19

19

20

21

22

Repeat steps 56-60 of *Peacock 1*.

Repeat steps 64-81 of *Peacock 1*.

23

Inside reverse-fold the flaps on both sides

24

Tuck in the center layer.

25

Crimp the outer layers (wings) only, so that the model stands on its wings and legs.

Finished.

Miura-ori and tessellation

The tail of *Peacock* has the same structure as **Miura-ori**, a crease pattern devised by Koryo Miura. Though the angles are different, compositions of mountain and valley creases are the same.

Although well known for map folding, Miura-ori was originally invented in space engineering technology to transport a large flat structure (such as an antenna, a solar panel, or a solar sail that receive the pressure of particles emitted from the Sun) into outer space. This structure is technically called **developable double corrugation surface** because it can be easily developed onto a plane.

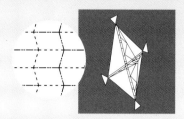

Miura-ori by Koryo Miura

This crease pattern itself had been used in lampshades and other designs before Miura started studying it and revealed its significance in engineering technology.

I designed, without the knowledge of Miura-ori, an earlier version of Peacock that has a similar crease pattern in its tail. It was folded from a rectangle. After learning and analyzing the Miura-ori, I came up with the idea of placing two sets of Miura-ori in different orientations within the square and connecting them at the right angle, thus resulting into this model.

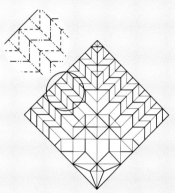

Peacock

As I discussed about the use of cuts in origami at the end of **Varieties of Origami**, models that use crease patterns that can be repeated infinitely, as with Miura-ori, are the ones that we can call true origami "with no cuts."

So, what will happen if we fold an infinitely large sheet in Miura-ori? The structure is called "double corrugation" because of the combination of horizontal and vertical pleats. But those two types of pleats are different. As you can see in the tail of Peacock, the sheet will be narrowed in one direction but become only slightly shorter in the other. When applied in engineering, it will be packed more compactly because the angles are closer to the right angle than 45° and 135° of Peacock. Still, because of the difference between the directions, the sheet becomes oblong when folded.

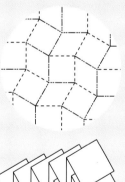

The difference also appears on the crease pattern. That can be eliminated by using two types of parallelograms, instead of one as in original Miura-ori. The first modeling of such extended Miura-ori is, as far as I know, **MARS** by Paulo Taborda Barreto.

For example, we can use squares and parallelograms whose angles are 60° and 120°. Then the folded pattern extends in all directions, though there is still a little difference between directions.

A pioneer of such tiling crease pattern, or **origami tessellation**, is Shuzo Fujimoto. He calls it "hira-ori", or flat-weaving, because folded patterns look as if it is woven. Recently it is also applied to the design of scales and other patterns.

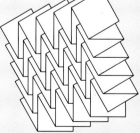

Extended Miura-ori: MARS by Paulo Taborda Barreto

Note that Miura-ori is also iso-area (see *Gift Box*).

Turkey

Theme: Self-similar

Difficult to fold using 6" (15 cm) origami paper. 10" (25 cm) to 12" (30 cm) very thin paper is suggested.

First, you need to decide how fine you would like to make the tail. That defines how many times you have to repeat the steps.

Repeat five times for the picture on the left and in the beginning of this book, though the diagram instructs to repeat three times.

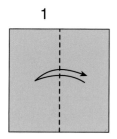

1

2

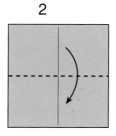

3

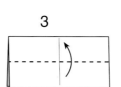

4

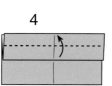

5

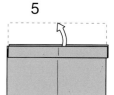

6

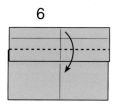

7

8

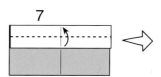

Fold the top layer only.

9

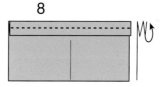

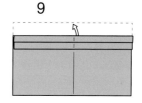

10

11

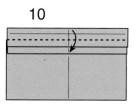

12

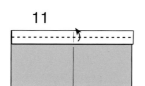

Fold the top layer only.

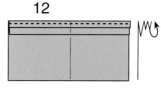

Repeat the steps if you want a finer tail.

13

14

15

16

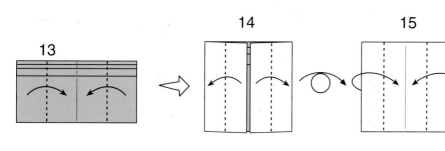

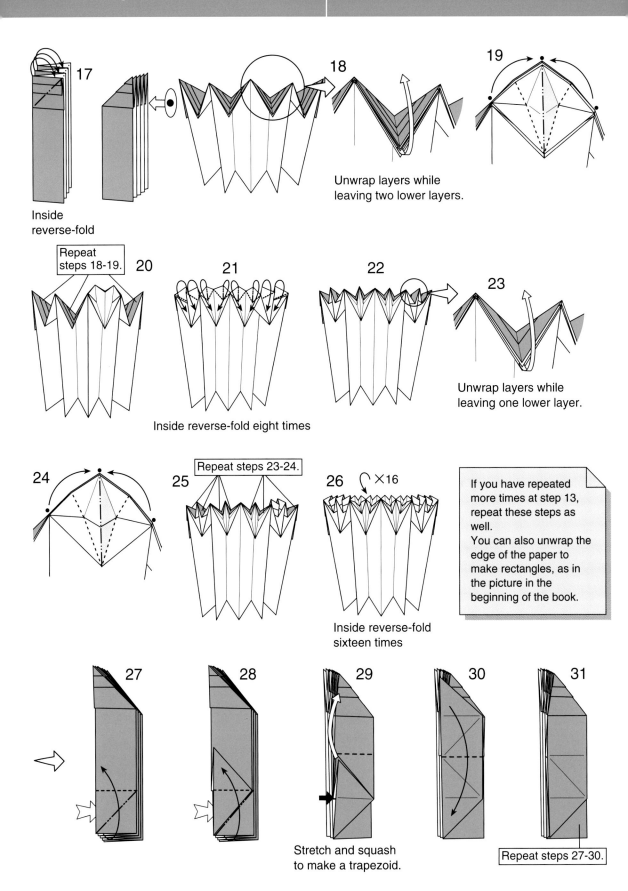

17

Inside
reverse-fold

18

Unwrap layers while
leaving two lower layers.

19

20 Repeat
steps 18-19.

21

22

23

Unwrap layers while
leaving one lower layer.

Inside reverse-fold eight times

24

25 Repeat steps 23-24.

26 ×16

Inside reverse-fold
sixteen times

If you have repeated
more times at step 13,
repeat these steps as
well.
You can also unwrap the
edge of the paper to
make rectangles, as in
the picture in the
beginning of the book.

27

28

29

Stretch and squash
to make a trapezoid.

30

31

Repeat steps 27-30.

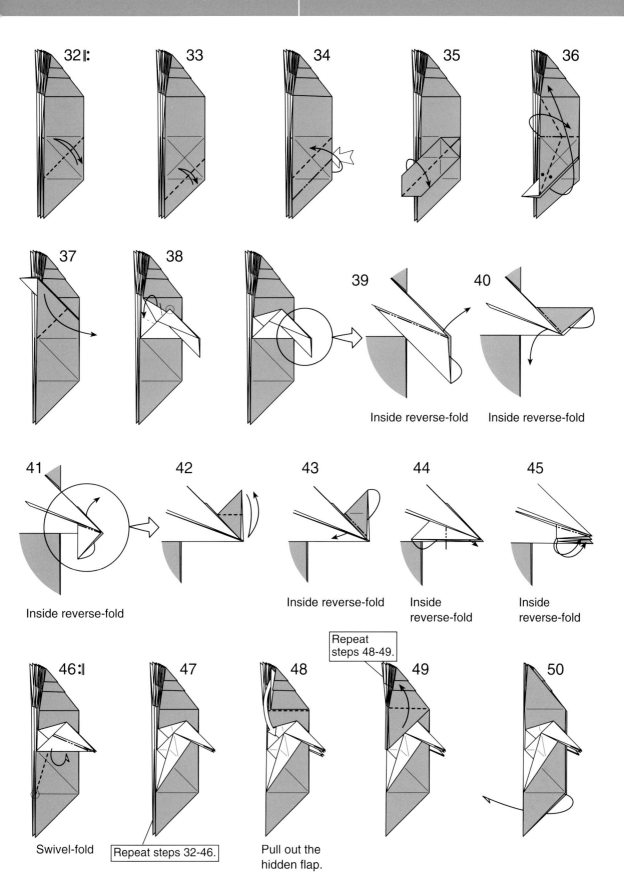

32

33

34

35

36

37

38

39

40

Inside reverse-fold

Inside reverse-fold

41

Inside reverse-fold

42

43

Inside reverse-fold

44

Inside reverse-fold

45

Inside reverse-fold

46

Swivel-fold

47

Repeat steps 32-46.

48

Pull out the hidden flap.

Repeat steps 48-49.

49

50

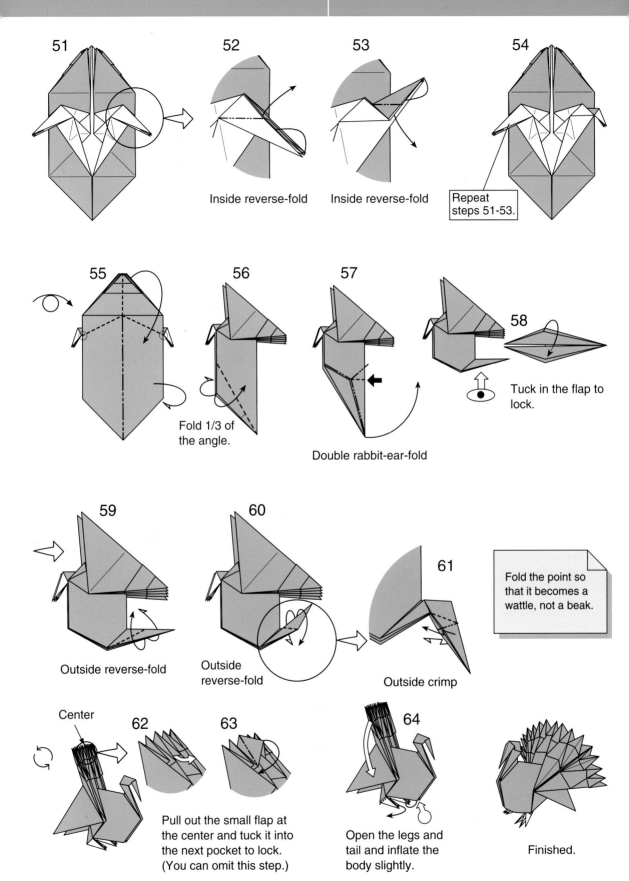

51

52

Inside reverse-fold

53

Inside reverse-fold

54

Repeat
steps 51-53.

55

56

Fold 1/3 of
the angle.

57

Double rabbit-ear-fold

58

Tuck in the flap to
lock.

59

Outside reverse-fold

60

Outside
reverse-fold

61

Outside crimp

Fold the point so
that it becomes a
wattle, not a beak.

Center

62

63

Pull out the small flap at
the center and tuck it into
the next pocket to lock.
(You can omit this step.)

64

Open the legs and
tail and inflate the
body slightly.

Finished.

Related model: *Surf*

Start from step 13 of *Turkey*.

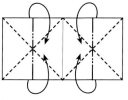

Fold two Water-bomb bases.

Repeat steps 18-26 of Turkey.

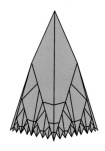

Self-similar and fractal

The main design aspect of *Turkey* is its repeating pattern at the tail. This pattern came from another model *Surf*, which is shown above.

I designed *Surf* not with an intention to design waves, but with a geometric interest in the crease pattern that repeat itself to branch infinitely.

Its basic structure is composed of the branches halving in the length and dividing into two, as shown on the right. The crease pattern is shown below. You can repeat the creases infinitely until the physical limitations of the paper.

This figure is an example of self-similar shape, which is a shape whose part is similar in proportion to the whole. The patterns of *Tree* and *Pyramid* are also self-similar. While those patterns are self-similar at one point, the pattern of this model is self-similar at an area with some length, that is, the ends of branches.

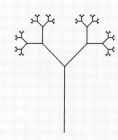

The basic structure

The notion of self-similar is one of the most important elements of fractal geometry.

In the crease patterns of *Surf* and *Turkey*, the total length of creases increases by the same amount at each step, because the number of creases becomes twice and the length of each one becomes half. Such "nested" branching structure is called sub-fractal in fractal geometry. This quasi-fractal structure is common in nature, plants like trees and cauliflowers, branches of rivers, and ramification of blood vessels.

Fractal geometry is not just a field of geometry but also a new viewpoint to recognize the nature, as the title of the book written by Benoît Mandelbrot, who is the advocator of fractal geometry, is *The Fractal Geometry of Nature*.

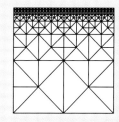

The crease pattern of Surf (mountain and valley folds are not shown).

While the father of the modern painting Paul Cézanne said, "treat nature by the cylinder, the sphere, the cone," Mandelbrot wrote that "Clouds are not spheres, mountains are not cones, coastlines are not circles, and bark is not smooth, nor does lightning travel in a straight line." I am not saying that Cézanne was wrong. In fact, I privately call my own cone-based model *Penguin* "Cézanne origami" and am arrogantly self-satisfied. But it is also true that the design with self-similar repeating patterns is wonderfully interesting, in a little different way from the design with solid bodies such as with cylinders and cones. And some of such designs are truly "origami-like."

Tyrannosaurus

Theme: Realism

Difficult to fold using 6" (15 cm) origami paper.
10" (25 cm) or larger paper is suggested.

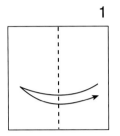
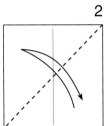
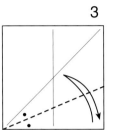
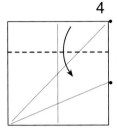
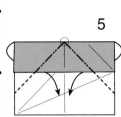

Inside reverse-fold

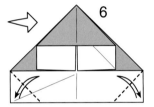
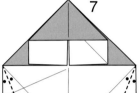
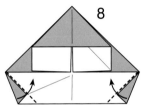
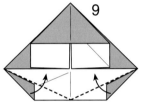

Realism in origami

I published a *Tyrannosaurus* in the past. But now I am ashamed of that model. It is partly because I failed to adopt the knowledge of current paleontology, but also because I made many mistakes that are just out of the question. Although it may have been inevitable that the model has the tail dropping down like a kangaroo, I would say it is a model of another species of dinosaur because it had three fingers at each foreleg, which was even emphasized in that design. In this version of Tyrannosaurus, I aimed for realism, though somewhat deformed.

Living creatures is the most popular theme in origami. One cannot deny that, in addition to the richness of geometry, the diversity of forms in the creatures and natural world is an inexhaustible source of origami design.

However, I always feel that the important thing is not only to pursue realism using techniques and skills. I personally give priority to the ideas of geometric design over the intention of making realistic models. My main priority for design is to achieve balance between "mitate" and geometry. That may be the definition of the notion of "origami-like" for me.

At the same time, I think other factors also define "origami-like." For example, capturing the characteristics of the subject with only one or two strokes, as in sketches, is also one of the ideals of origami design. But such models inevitably contain many "judgment folds" that decrease the geometric interest. That is annoying for me.

Another factor that defines origami design is the diagramming. I prefer such a design that folders can reproduce obtaining the same result by following the diagrams. This condition often enhances the quality of design rather than compromises it.

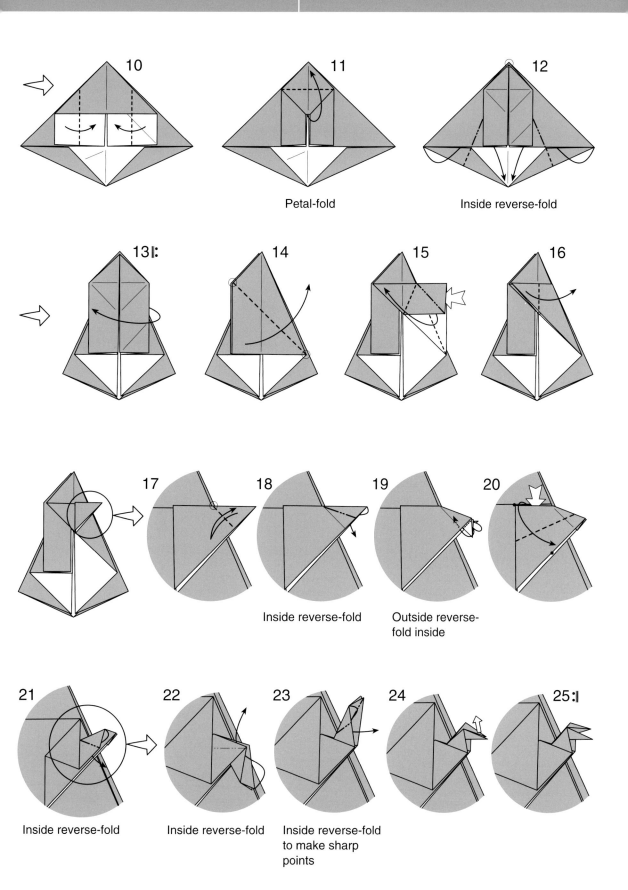

10

11

Petal-fold

12

Inside reverse-fold

13

14

15

16

17

18

Inside reverse-fold

19

Outside reverse-
fold inside

20

21

Inside reverse-fold

22

Inside reverse-fold

23

Inside reverse-fold
to make sharp
points

24

25

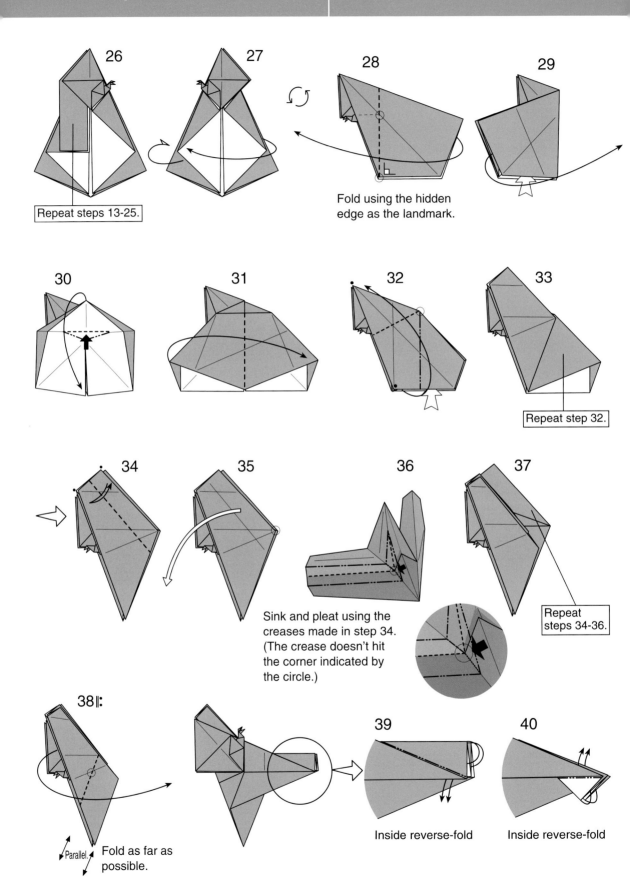

26

27

Repeat steps 13-25.

28

Fold using the hidden
edge as the landmark.

29

30

31

32

33

Repeat step 32.

34

35

36

Sink and pleat using the
creases made in step 34.
(The crease doesn't hit
the corner indicated by
the circle.)

37

Repeat
steps 34-36.

38 ‖:

Parallel. Fold as far as
possible.

39

Inside reverse-fold

40

Inside reverse-fold

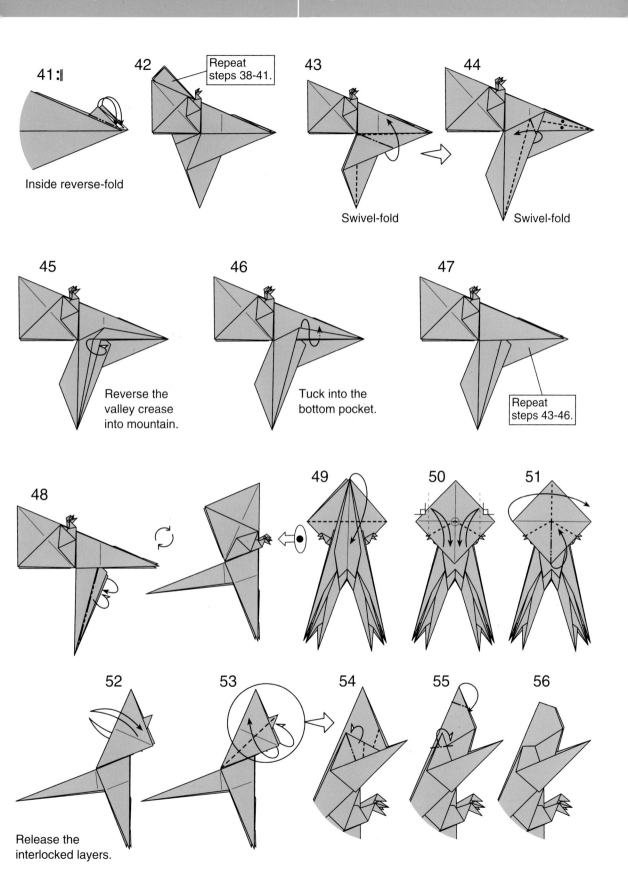

41: Inside reverse-fold

42 Repeat steps 38-41.

43 Swivel-fold

44 Swivel-fold

45 Reverse the valley crease into mountain.

46 Tuck into the bottom pocket.

47 Repeat steps 43-46.

48 Release the interlocked layers.

49

50

51

52

53

54

55

56

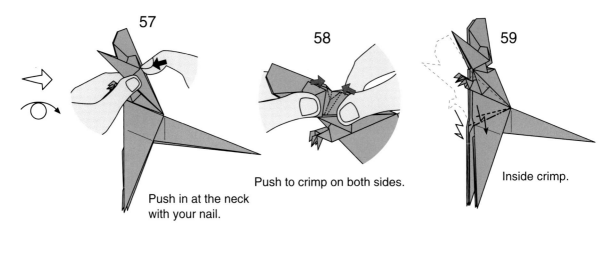

57 Push in at the neck with your nail.

58 Push to crimp on both sides.

59 Inside crimp.

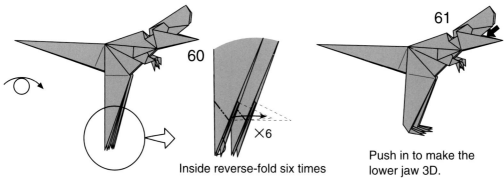

60 Inside reverse-fold six times ×6

61 Push in to make the lower jaw 3D.

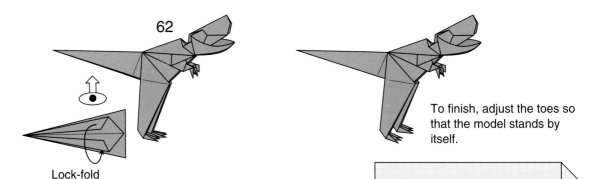

62 Lock-fold

To finish, adjust the toes so that the model stands by itself.

If you shape the legs, the model becomes alive but difficult to stand by itself.

You can add some more shaping, such as pinching the legs, to make the model three-dimensional. But I prefer stopping here.

It is very difficult to decide where to stop folding. That may be an eternal problem in origami design.

Anyway, I think it is more important to make the model stand by itself than to shape it well.

Eastern Dragon

Theme: Grafting

Not impossible to fold using 6" (15 cm) origami paper. 10" (25 cm) or larger thin washi (Japanese handmade paper) is suggested.

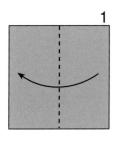
1

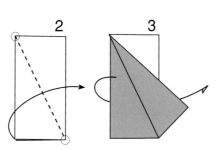
2   3

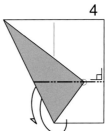
4

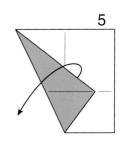
5

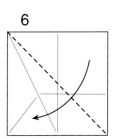
6

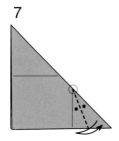
7

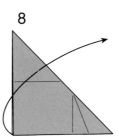
8

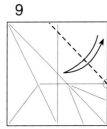
9

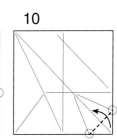
10

Grafting technique

I designed this *Eastern Dragon* by adding craws to my previous design. This technique is a kind of **preparation** explained in *Three-headed Crane*.

The gray area in the crease pattern shown on the right indicates the grafted part. I added a "gusset" while leaving the original crease pattern intact.

As a side effect of adding the craws, I also obtained a longer body.

Note that an area can be grafted not only along the sides of the square, as in this model, but also in different parts.

You can divide an existing crease pattern and insert a gusset between them. *Devil* is an example, where fingers are grafted into the original model.

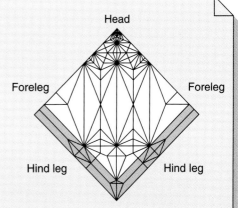

The crease pattern of *Eastern Dragon* (mountain and valley folds are not shown).

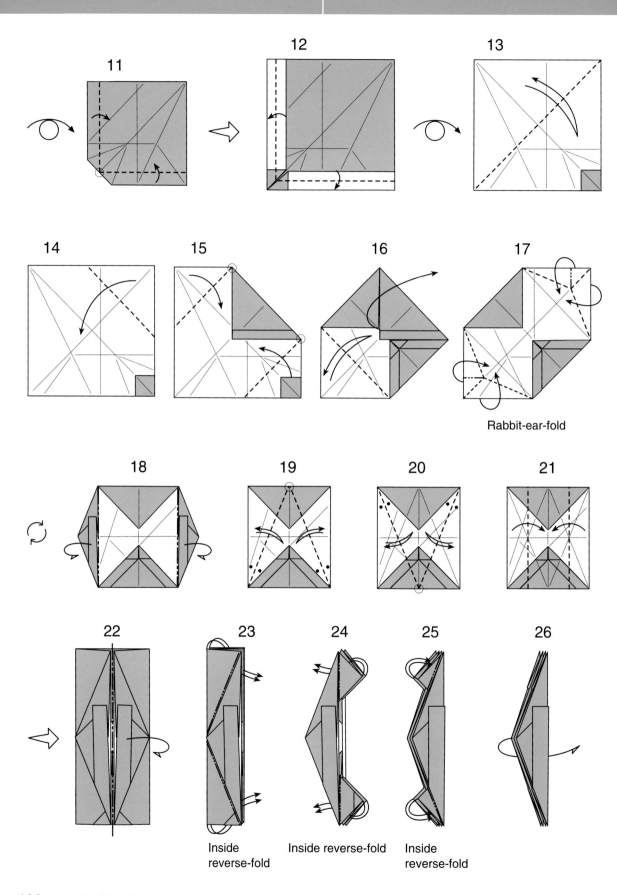

Rabbit-ear-fold

Inside
reverse-fold

Inside reverse-fold

Inside
reverse-fold

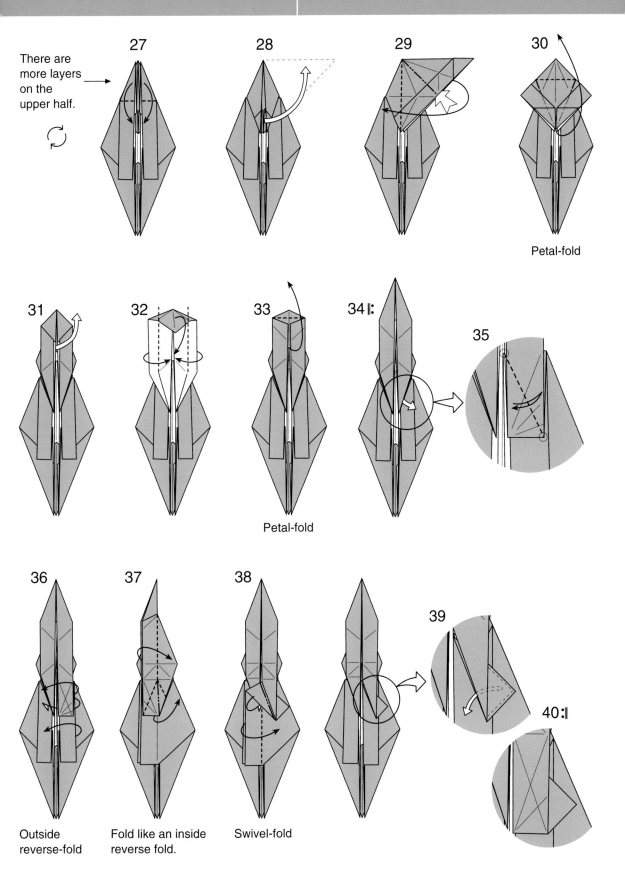

27

There are more layers on the upper half.

28

29

30

Petal-fold

31

32

33

34

35

Petal-fold

36

37

38

39

40

Outside reverse-fold

Fold like an inside reverse fold.

Swivel-fold

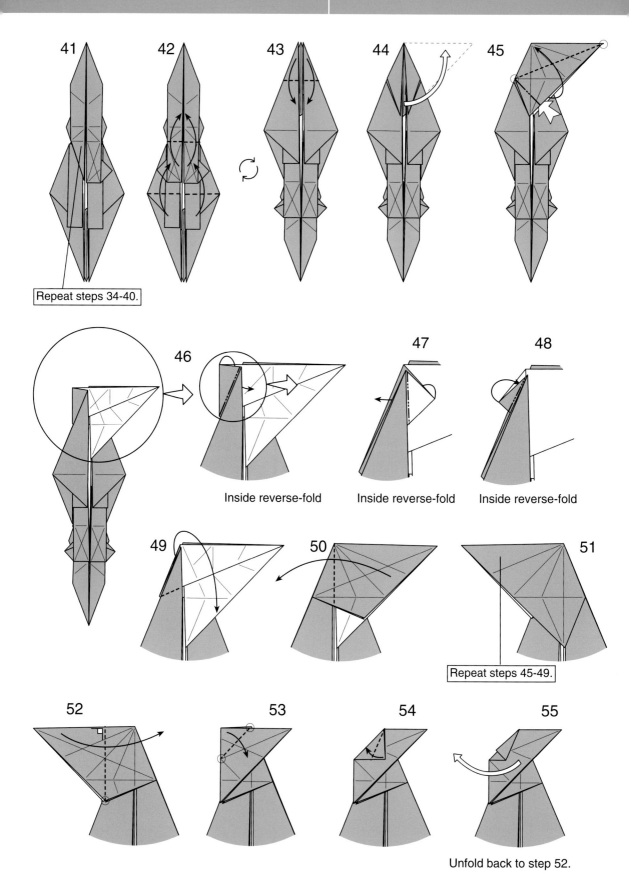

41

42

43

44

45

Repeat steps 34-40.

46

47

48

Inside reverse-fold

Inside reverse-fold

Inside reverse-fold

49

50

51

Repeat steps 45-49.

52

53

54

55

Unfold back to step 52.

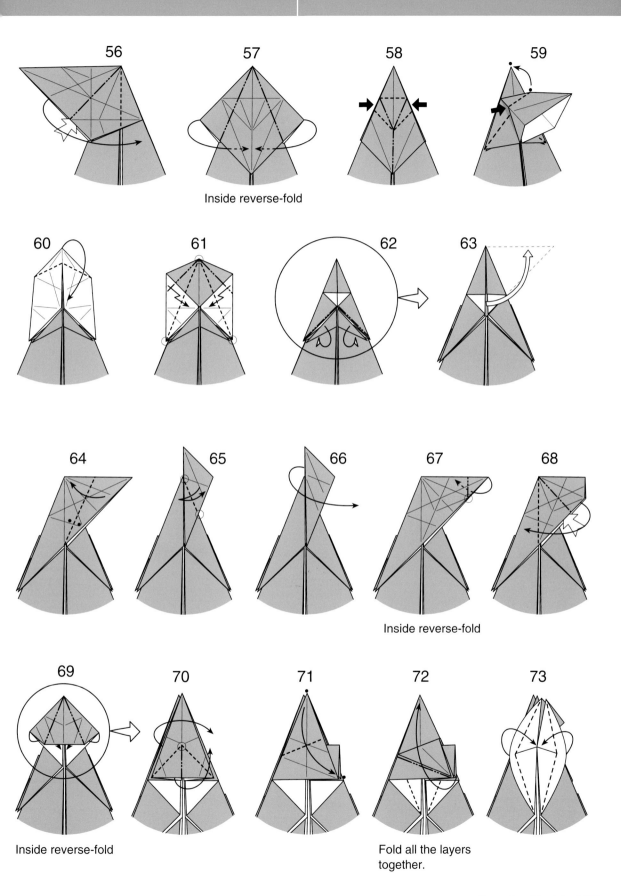

56

57

58
Inside reverse-fold

59

60

61

62

63

64

65

66

67

68
Inside reverse-fold

69
Inside reverse-fold

70

71

72
Fold all the layers together.

73

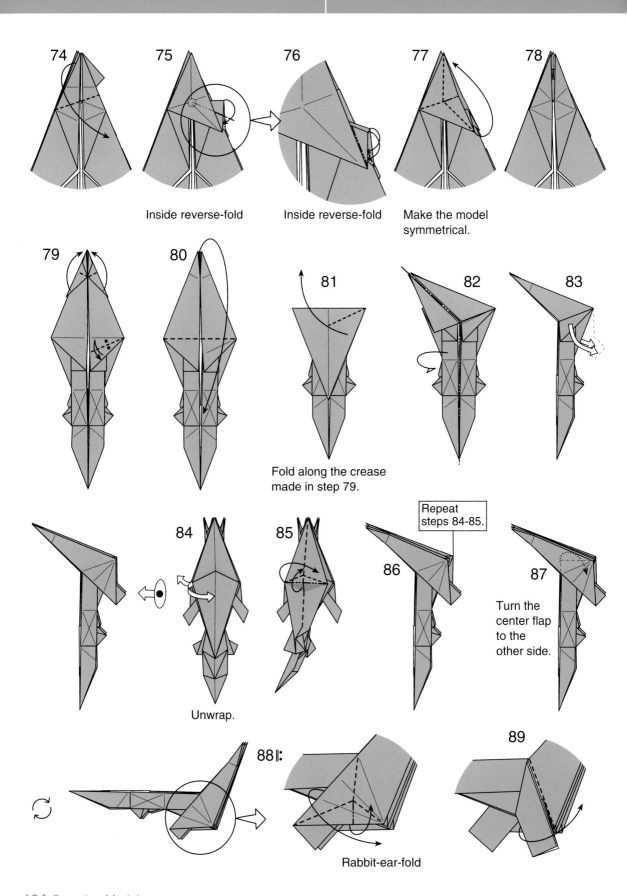

74

75

76

Inside reverse-fold

Inside reverse-fold

77

Make the model symmetrical.

78

79

80

81

Fold along the crease made in step 79.

82

83

84

Unwrap.

85

Repeat steps 84-85.

86

87

Turn the center flap to the other side.

88

Rabbit-ear-fold

89

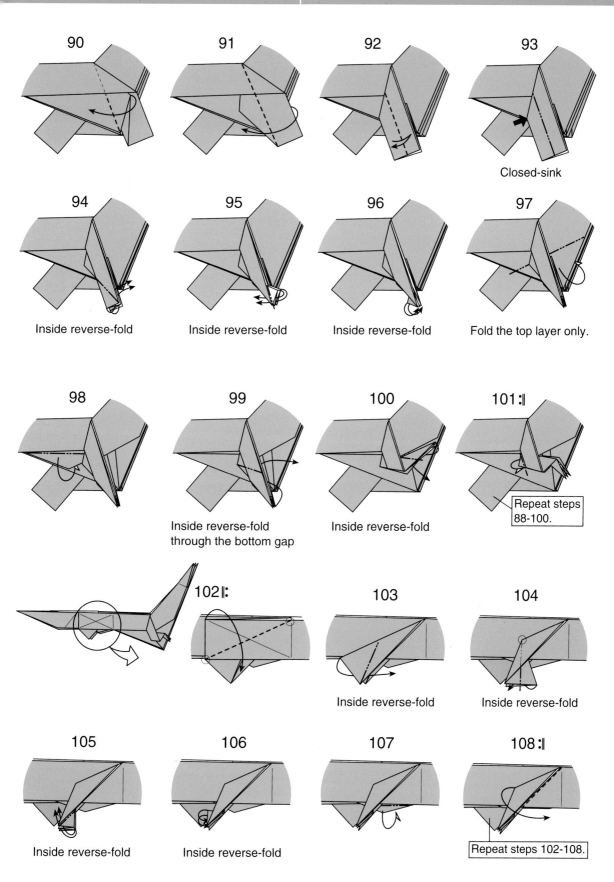

90

91

92

93

Closed-sink

94

Inside reverse-fold

95

Inside reverse-fold

96

Inside reverse-fold

97

Fold the top layer only.

98

99

Inside reverse-fold
through the bottom gap

100

Inside reverse-fold

101 :‖

Repeat steps
88-100.

102 ‖:

103

Inside reverse-fold

104

Inside reverse-fold

105

Inside reverse-fold

106

Inside reverse-fold

107

108 :‖

Repeat steps 102-108.

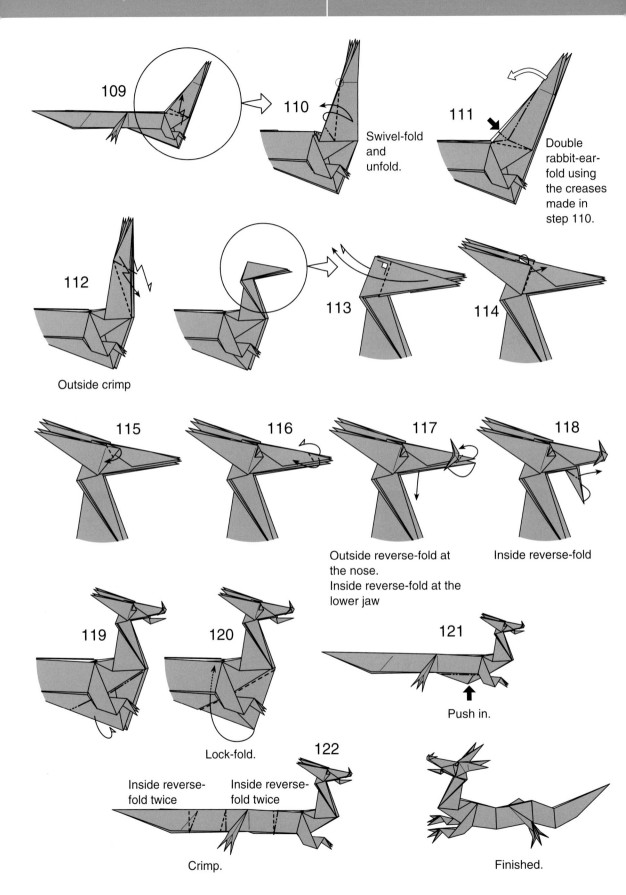

109

110 Swivel-fold and unfold.

111 Double rabbit-ear-fold using the creases made in step 110.

112 Outside crimp

113

114

115

116

117 Outside reverse-fold at the nose.
Inside reverse-fold at the lower jaw

118 Inside reverse-fold

119

120 Lock-fold.

121 Push in.

122 Crimp.

Inside reverse-fold twice   Inside reverse-fold twice

Finished.

Samurai Helmet Beetle

Theme: No glue, no cuts

Difficult to fold using 6" (15 cm) origami paper. 12" (30 cm) paper is suggested.

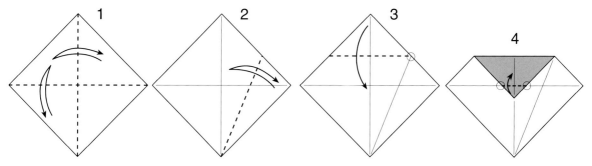

1   2   3   4

Symbolism of the "glue"

This model is a modified version of my *Flying Samurai Helmet Beetle*, which was designed about 10 years ago for an informal competition known as the "Bug Wars." At that time I intended it as a negative Mannerism or a kind of joke, using excessive techniques, artificiality, and exaggeration. But now I think it was not a bad model at all.

In fact, the model did not require extremely thin paper to fold as long as the sheet was large enough, nor did it require glue to keep its shape. In improving the model, I paid more attention to in addition not to require glue also not to tear easily.

I deliberately avoid glue with the models in this book, as I used lock folds in some models.

The crease pattern of Samurai Helmet Beetle (mountain and valley folds are not shown).

Sometimes the selling point of an origami model is "folded without cuts or glue." Setting aside cuts, "no glue" appears to imply that the model is not folded from multiple sheets. However, requiring no glue to keep its shape is one of the ideals even for a model folded from one sheet.

If you do not use glue, you can unfold a finished model completely to show that it is folded from a single sheet. That may seem to be an unnatural reasoning. But the fact that the origami model can be restored anytime to a plain sheet symbolizes "openness" of the wonder of how it was made, which is one of the fascination in origami.

Moreover, creases on paper have a natural tendency to unfold. "No glue" means try to keep creases just by folding. It also symbolizes the recognition of the physical nature of the paper.

However, using glue does not always compromise origami designs. What is important is that the design centers on the "folded shape" or "bended surfaces emerged from a plane". Speaking of bended surfaces, when we design an origami model according to the composition of points, as in this *Samurai Helmet Beetle*, most of the surfaces are folded inside and hidden from the outline of the model. Therefore, one can say that the point of such model is in its folding, or unfolding, sequence rather than the finished shape.

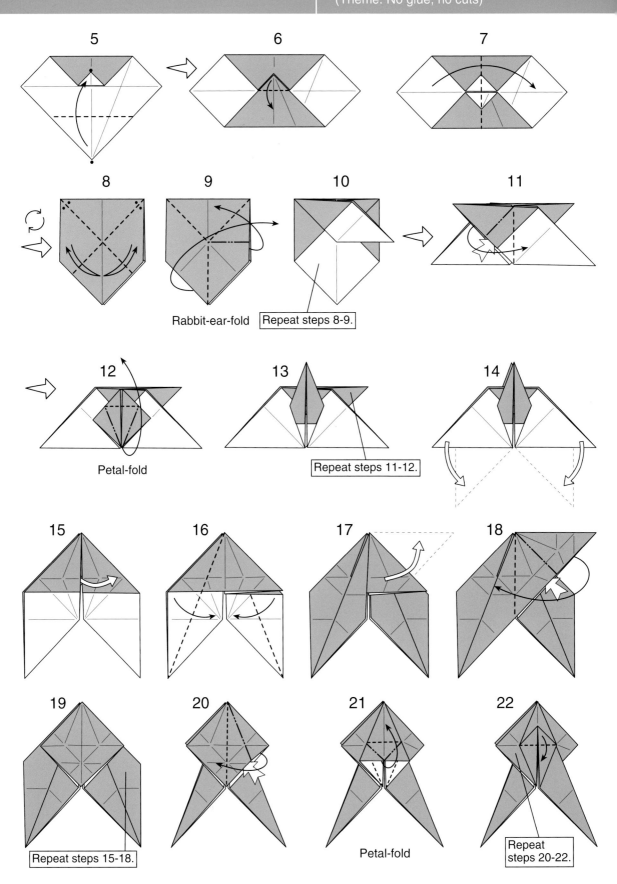

5

6

7

8

9

10

Rabbit-ear-fold

Repeat steps 8-9.

11

12

Petal-fold

13

Repeat steps 11-12.

14

15

16

17

18

19

Repeat steps 15-18.

20

21

Petal-fold

22

Repeat
steps 20-22.

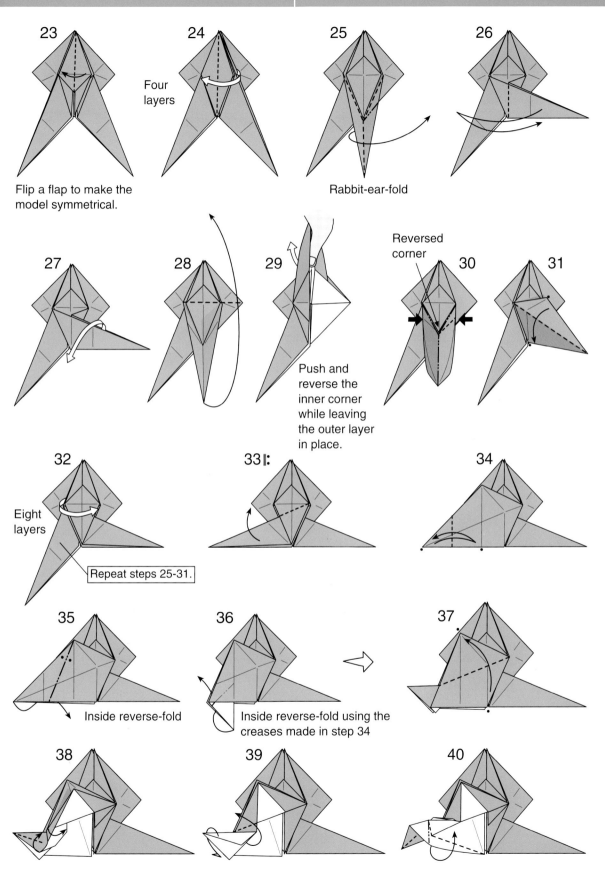

23 Flip a flap to make the model symmetrical.

24 Four layers

25 Rabbit-ear-fold

26

27

28

29 Push and reverse the inner corner while leaving the outer layer in place.

30 Reversed corner

31

32 Eight layers

Repeat steps 25-31.

33

34

35 Inside reverse-fold

36 Inside reverse-fold using the creases made in step 34

37

38

39

40

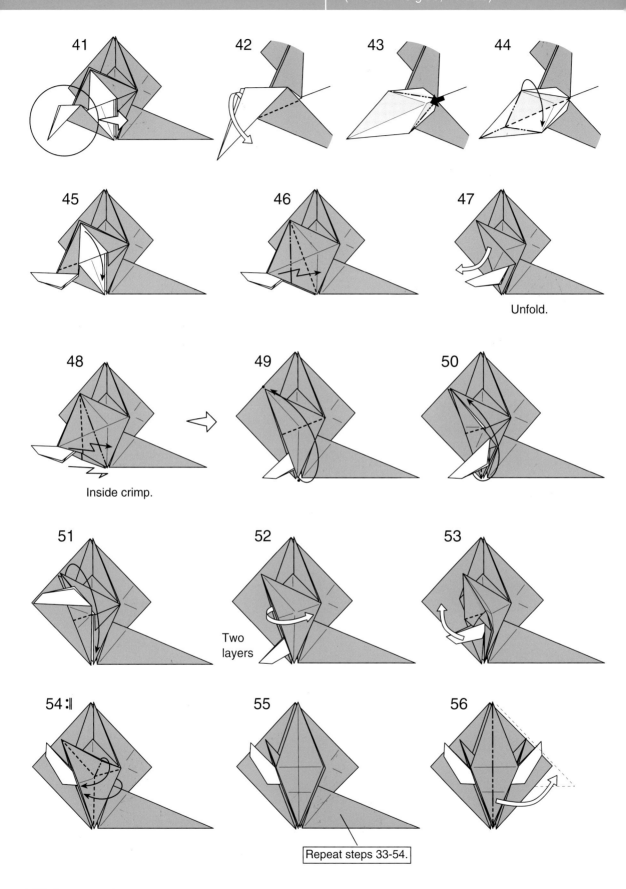

41

42

43

44

45

46

47

Unfold.

48

Inside crimp.

49

50

51

52

Two
layers

53

54 :‖

55

56

Repeat steps 33-54.

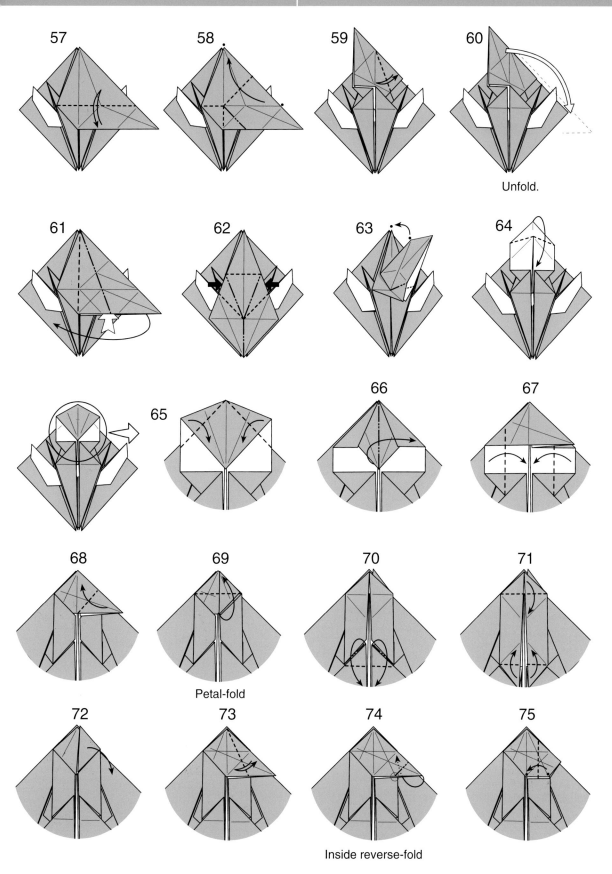

57

58

59

60

Unfold.

61

62

63

64

65

66

67

68

69

Petal-fold

70

71

72

73

74

75

Inside reverse-fold

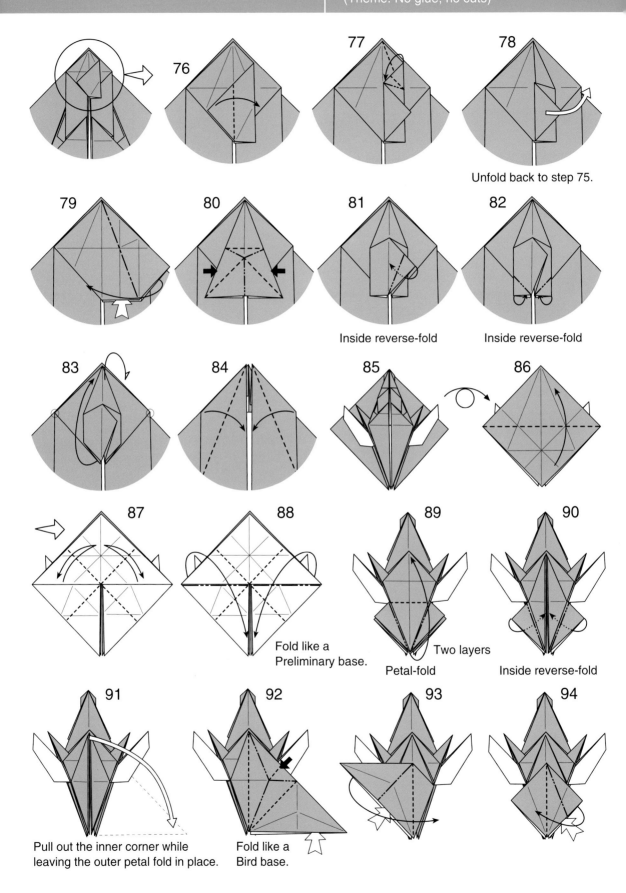

76

77

78

Unfold back to step 75.

79

80

81

82

Inside reverse-fold

Inside reverse-fold

83

84

85

86

87

88

Fold like a
Preliminary base.

89

Two layers

Petal-fold

90

Inside reverse-fold

91

Pull out the inner corner while
leaving the outer petal fold in place.

92

Fold like a
Bird base.

93

94

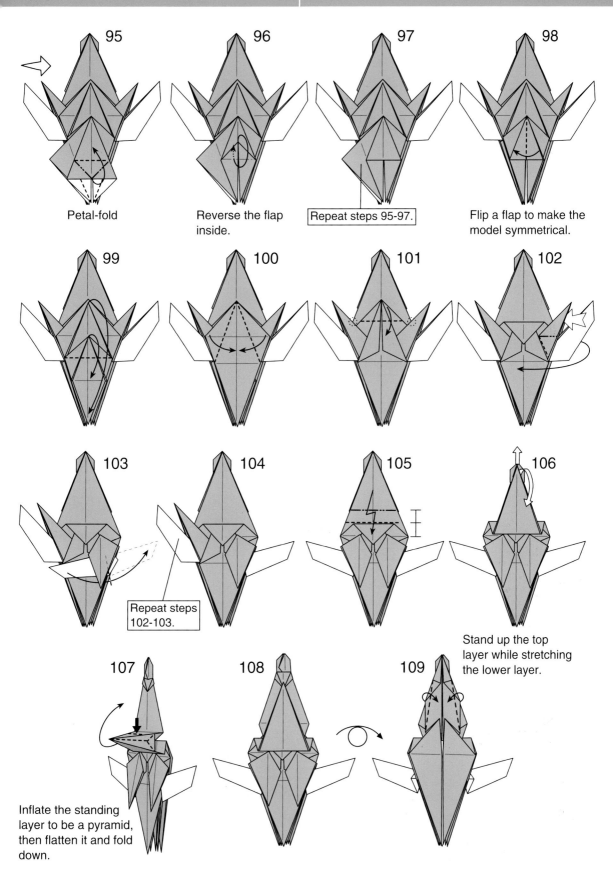

95 Petal-fold

96 Reverse the flap inside.

97 Repeat steps 95-97.

98 Flip a flap to make the model symmetrical.

99

100

101

102

103

104 Repeat steps 102-103.

105

106 Stand up the top layer while stretching the lower layer.

107 Inflate the standing layer to be a pyramid, then flatten it and fold down.

108

109

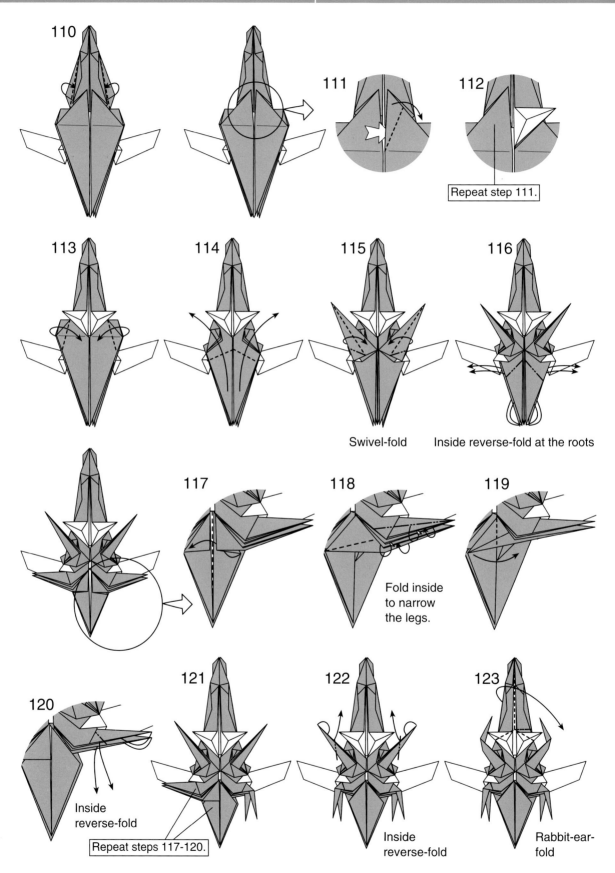

110

111

112

Repeat step 111.

113

114

115

116

Swivel-fold   Inside reverse-fold at the roots

117

118

Fold inside
to narrow
the legs.

119

120

Inside
reverse-fold

Repeat steps 117-120.

121

122

Inside
reverse-fold

123

Rabbit-ear-
fold

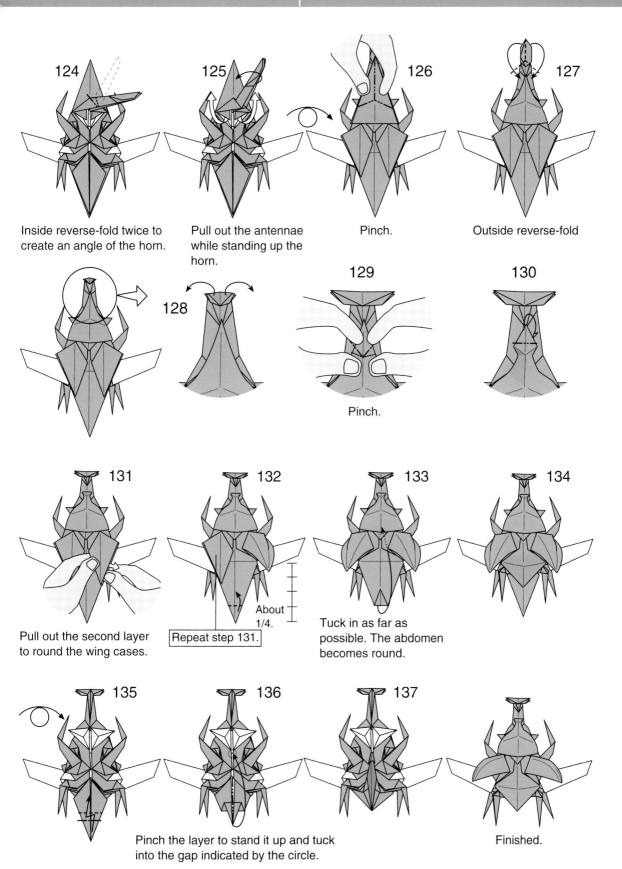

124 Inside reverse-fold twice to create an angle of the horn.

125 Pull out the antennae while standing up the horn.

126 Pinch.

127 Outside reverse-fold

128

129 Pinch.

130

131 Pull out the second layer to round the wing cases.

132 About 1/4. Repeat step 131.

133 Tuck in as far as possible. The abdomen becomes round.

134

135 Pinch the layer to stand it up and tuck into the gap indicated by the circle.

136

137 Finished.

Devil

Theme: Taming the devil

Difficult to fold using 6" (15 cm) origami paper.
10" (25 cm) or larger paper is suggested.

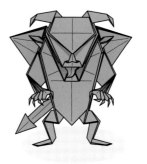

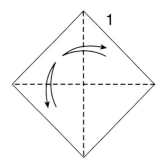

1

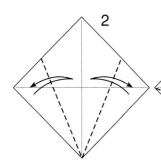

2

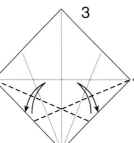

3

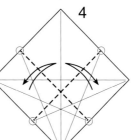

4

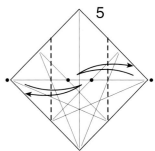

5

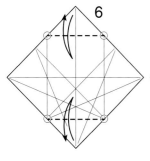

6

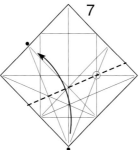

7

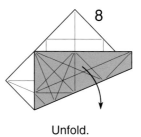

8

Unfold.

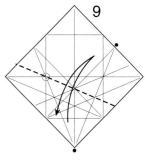

9

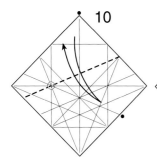

10

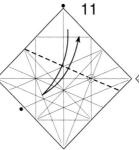

11

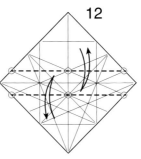

12

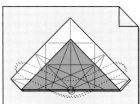

Fold so that the creases indicated by the dotted line align in step 12, as well as in steps 14 and 15.

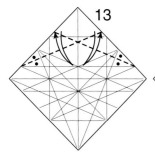

13

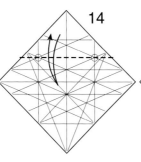

14

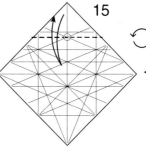

15

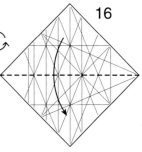

16

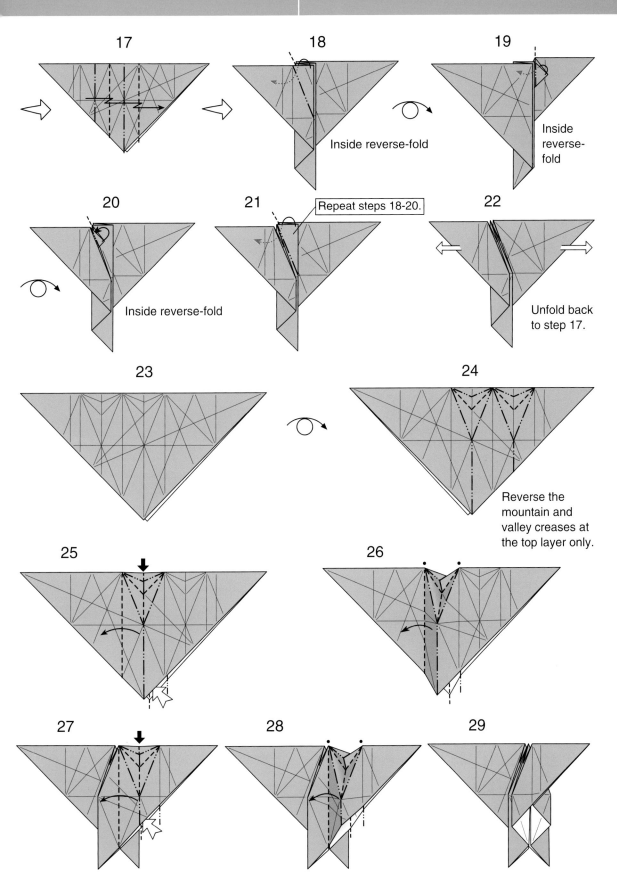

17

18

Inside reverse-fold

19

Inside reverse-fold

20

Inside reverse-fold

21

Repeat steps 18-20.

22

Unfold back to step 17.

23

24

Reverse the mountain and valley creases at the top layer only.

25

26

27

28

29

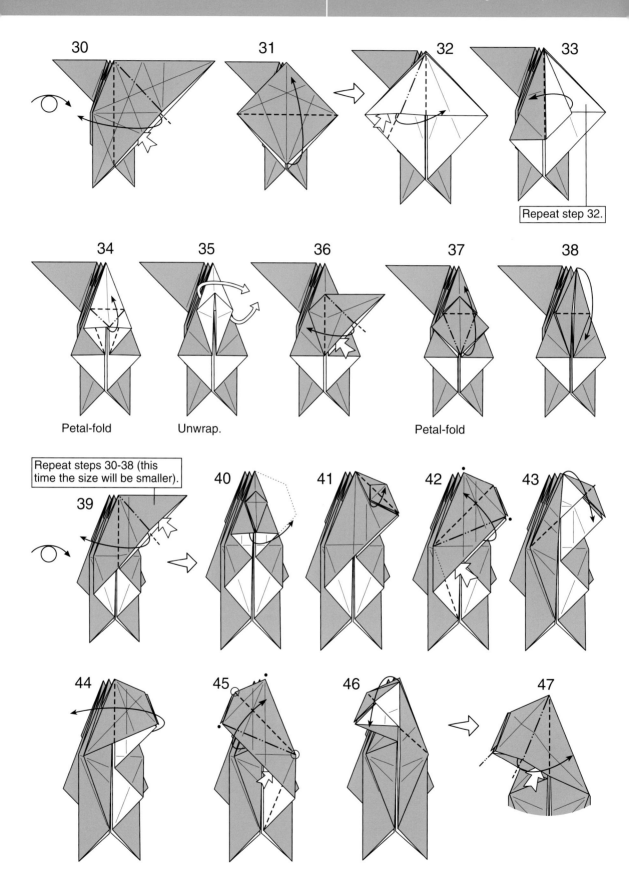

30

31

32

33

Repeat step 32.

34

35

36

37

38

Petal-fold

Unwrap.

Petal-fold

Repeat steps 30-38 (this time the size will be smaller).

39

40

41

42

43

44

45

46

47

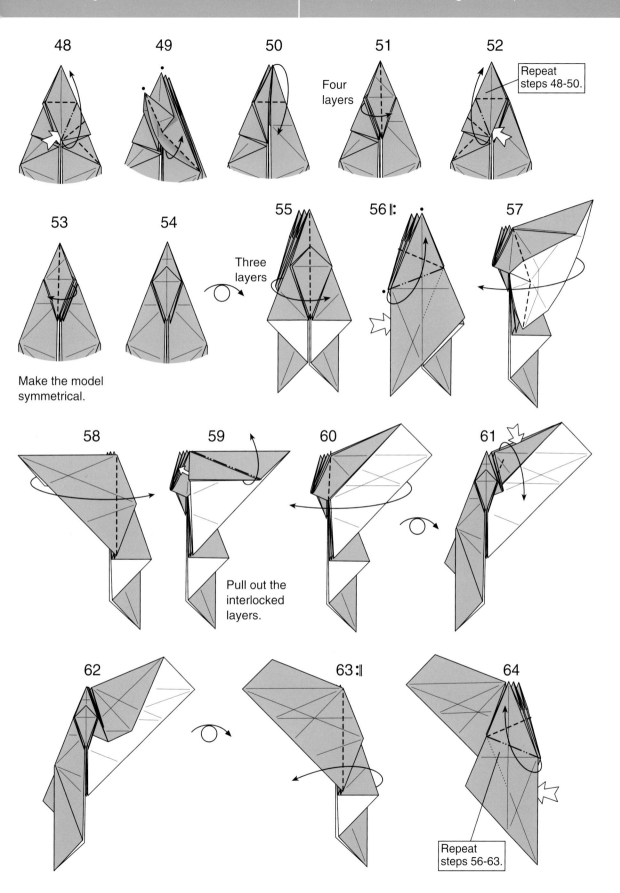

48

49

50

51

Four
layers

52

Repeat
steps 48-50.

53

54

Make the model
symmetrical.

Three
layers

55

56

57

58

59

Pull out the
interlocked
layers.

60

61

62

63

64

Repeat
steps 56-63.

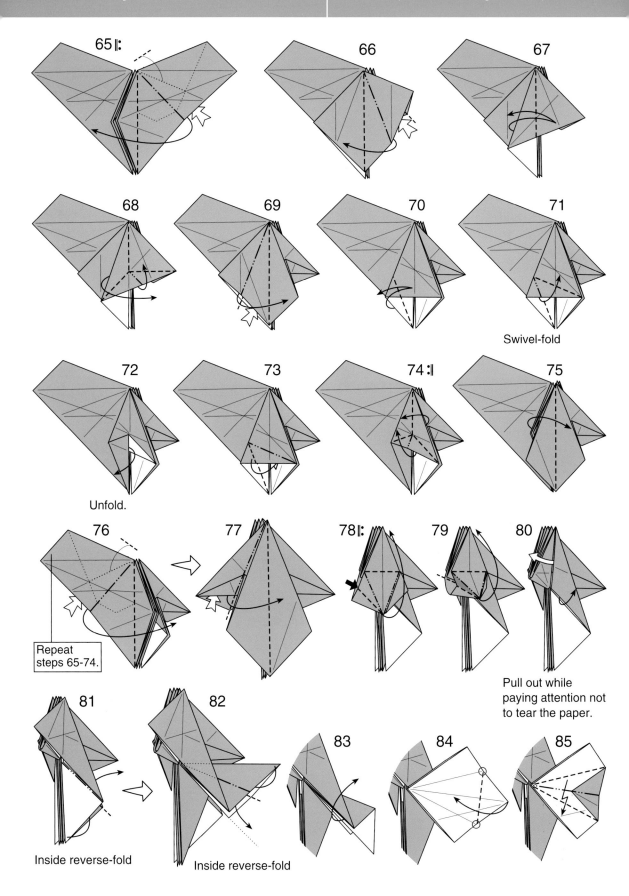

65 ‖:

66

67

68

69

70

71

Swivel-fold

72

Unfold.

73

74 :‖

75

76

Repeat
steps 65-74.

77

78 ‖:

79

80

Pull out while
paying attention not
to tear the paper.

81

82

Inside reverse-fold

Inside reverse-fold

83

84

85

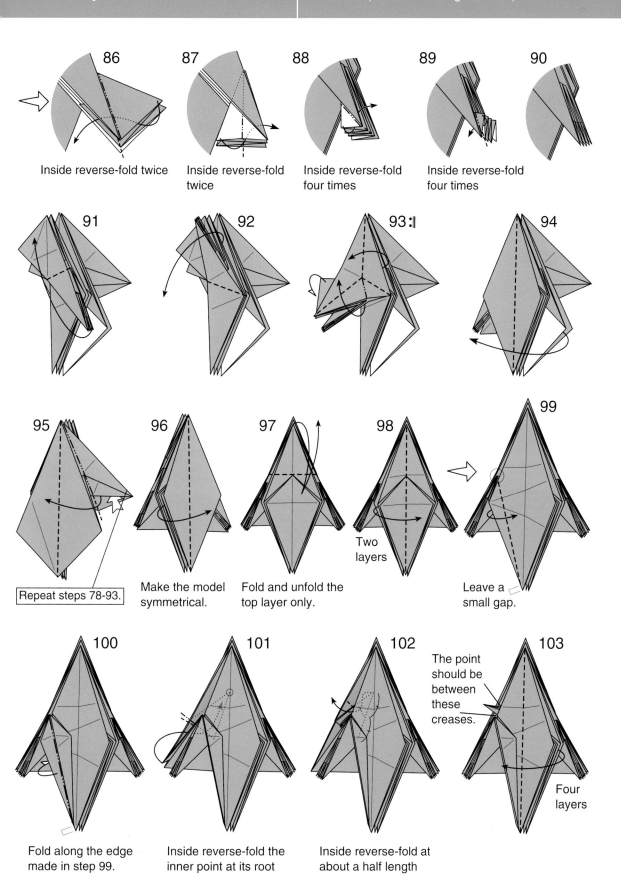

86 Inside reverse-fold twice

87 Inside reverse-fold twice

88 Inside reverse-fold four times

89 Inside reverse-fold four times

90

91

92

93:‖

94

95 Repeat steps 78-93.

96 Make the model symmetrical.

97 Fold and unfold the top layer only.

98 Two layers

99 Leave a small gap.

100 Fold along the edge made in step 99.

101 Inside reverse-fold the inner point at its root

102 Inside reverse-fold at about a half length

103 The point should be between these creases.

Four layers

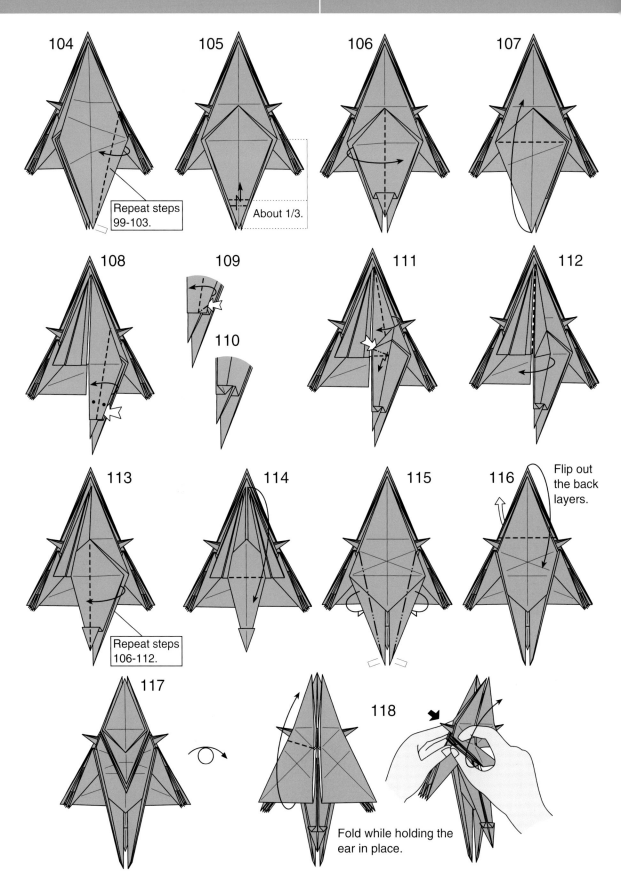

104

Repeat steps 99-103.

105

About 1/3.

106

107

108

109

110

111

112

113

Repeat steps 106-112.

114

115

116

Flip out the back layers.

117

118

Fold while holding the ear in place.

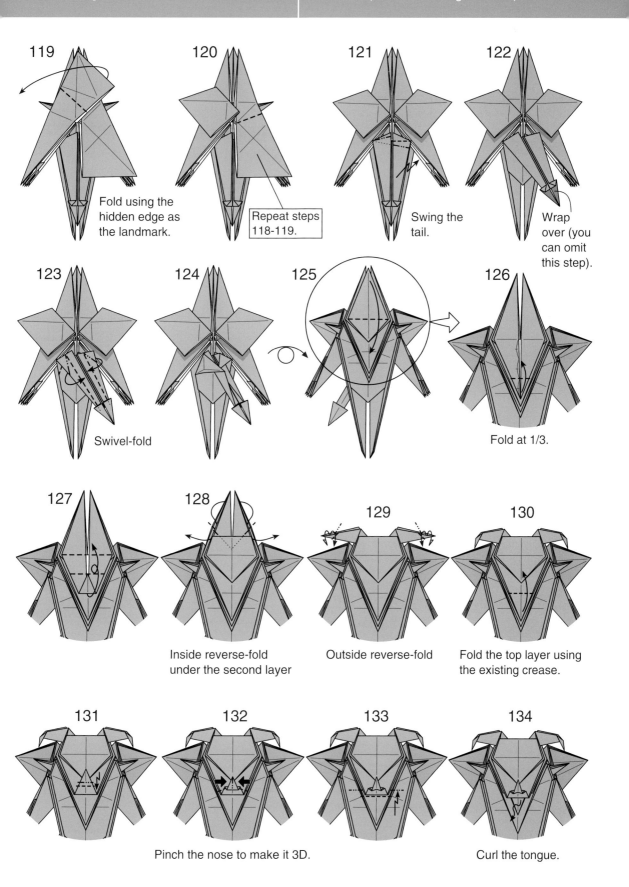

119 Fold using the hidden edge as the landmark.

120 Repeat steps 118-119.

121 Swing the tail.

122 Wrap over (you can omit this step).

123 Swivel-fold

124

125

126 Fold at 1/3.

127

128 Inside reverse-fold under the second layer

129 Outside reverse-fold

130 Fold the top layer using the existing crease.

131

132 Pinch the nose to make it 3D.

133

134 Curl the tongue.

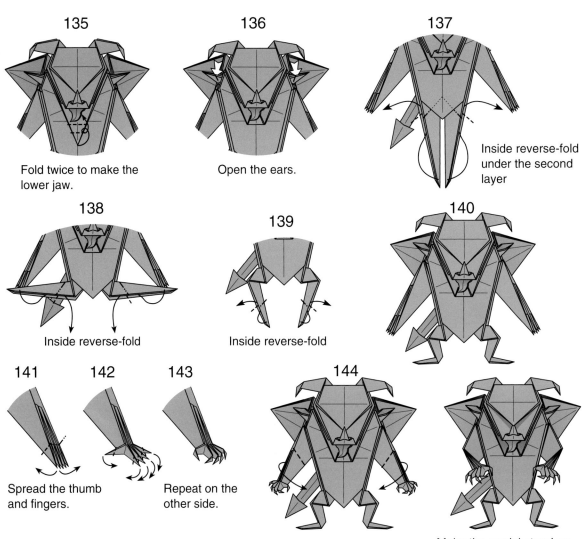

135

Fold twice to make the lower jaw.

136

Open the ears.

137

Inside reverse-fold under the second layer

138

Inside reverse-fold

139

Inside reverse-fold

140

141   **142**   **143**

Spread the thumb and fingers.

Repeat on the other side.

144

Make the model stand on its legs and the tail to finish.

This *Devil* is my first published model (published in the appendix of *Nikkei Science* in 1980). At the same time, it is my masterwork.

The fact that my masterpiece is a quarter of a century old may indicate that my origami has not developed since then. But now I feel this model to be more a kind of objective theorem of geometry than just a model of mine.

My design note at that time was titled "An emotional study on division of the plane and superposition of paper." Though it is too pretentious, typical of the young I was at the time, I still think the title do not miss the target.

To play with a material called paper, based on geometry, but sensuously rather than analytically. That seems to be the long-standing fascination of origami for me.

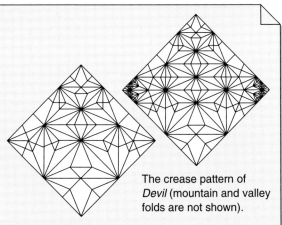

The crease pattern of *Devil* (mountain and valley folds are not shown).

The crease pattern of *Devil* (without the fingers) (mountain and valley folds are not shown).

◈ Afterword ◈

I express my gratitude to Kunihiko Kasahara who has carved out my way to origami (although carving is not a welcome term in origami), Tomoko Fuse who has been insisted on my writing a book for a number of years and strongly recommended me to the publisher, the mystery writer Yukito Ayatsuji who has contributed a blurb for this book, and all of my origami friends mentioned or not mentioned in this book.

I made the diagrams myself using a computer and an illustration software. Though I had some experiences before, I became fully aware of the shortcomings of my diagrams while creating a significant amount of them. During the process, I was always inspired by the diagrams created by Hideo Komatsu. In fact, the diagram of *Devil* is based on his diagrams. For the other models, I reviewed all of them specifically for this book, including the models that I had published before, and created new diagrams.

I also thank the editor Yasushi Takado, the photographer Kazuhisa Okuyama, the designer Fukura Yanagihara, the printer Takahiro Toyama at Kato Bummei-sha, and others who have helped me in making this book.

And my wife Sumiko, you are not just one of my origami friends but the one I owe the greatest gratitude. If you did not say, "I want to see your new book," I, who lacks persistence, would never have written a whole book on the pretense of being busy. You were also the most "suitable" proofreader of the diagrams as you are not the best but not the worst folder.

Well, such formal and personal statements may be boring for readers. But I found, while making this book, that I became more and more willing to share my personal "Eureka!" (I have found it!) with many people.

It has already been a quarter of a century since I published my models in *Viva! Origami* edited by Kasahara, when I was in my early 20s. The book has already been unavailable for many years, and I have heard that many people want to see it republished. I publish in this book a few models from the previous one with new diagrams. I also rewrote the theories of technical folding and other topics to include the new knowledge acquired since then. I am not sure if a quarter of a century is long or short, but I am sure I have always been enjoying inexhaustible pleasure of origami during that period.

Today's origami world has developed much wider and deeper, based on the accomplishments of pioneers and increase of emerging talents. In this book, I tried to describe, using my models, a broad fascination of origami from my point of view.
However, there are several other topics that are not included in this book, such as action models that you can play with, models that have practical use, curved creases, relationship with computational sciences, and a number of shaping techniques for displaying models. Still, I believe that this book is rich in its contents. Some pages have so much content that the diagrams look over-crowded.
Anyway, I hope readers of this book will fully enjoy the attractive play of origami, where mathematics, culture, and art are on the same plane.

◈ Index ◈

◈ References ◈

Maekawa, Jun, Kasahara, Kunihiko ed. *Viva! Origami*, Sanrio 1983

Abe, hisashi *Sugoizo Origami*, Nippon Hyoronsha, 2003

Fuse, Tomoko *Hako-o Tsukuro Yunitto Origami*, Seibundo Shinkosha, 2000

Haga, Kazuo *Origamics 1*, Nippon Hyoronsha, 1999

Haga, Kazuo *Origamics 2*, Nippon Hyoronsha, 2005

Hull, Tom ed. *Origami* [3], A. K. Peters, 2002

Husimi, Kodi and Husimi, Mitsue *Origami-no Kikagaku* revised edition, Nippon Hyoronsha, 1984

Kamiya, Satoshi *Works of Satoshi Kamiya*, Origami House, 2005

Kasahara, Kunihiko *Origami Shinhakken 1*, Japan Publications, 2005

Kasahara, Kunihiko *Origami Shinhakken 2*, Japan Publications, 2005

Kasahara, Kunihiko *Origami Shinhakken 3*, Japan Publications, 2005

Kawahata, Fumiaki *Origami Fantasy*, Origami House, 1995

Kawamura, Miyuki *Tamentai-no Origami*, Nippon Hyoronsha, 1995

Kawasaki, Toshikazu *Bara-to Origami-to Sugaku-to*, Morikita Publishing, 1998

Lang, Robert J. *Origami Design Secrets*, A. K. Peters, 2003

Montroll, John *Origami Inside-out*, Antroll Publishing, 1993

Nishikawa, Seiji *Works of Seiji Nishikawa*, Origami House, 2003

Okamura, Masao *Tsunagi Orizuru-no Sekai*: *Renzuru-no Koten "Hiden Sembazuru Orikata"*, Honnoizumisya, 2006

Yamaguchi, Makoto and Tateishi, Koichi *Folding Japan with Origami in English*, Natsumesha, 2005

Yoshino, Issei *Issei Super Complex Origami*, Origami House, 1996

Yoshizawa, Akira *Inochi Yutakana Origami*, Sojusha, 1996

(The publication of Origami House is only available directly at www.origamihouse.jp)

Periodicals on Origami

Origami Tanteidan, Japan Origami Academic Society (bimonthly)

Origami, Nippon Origami Association (monthly)

Oru, Sojusha (no longer published)

Web-sites on Origami

Japan Origami Academic Society, http://www.origami.gr.jp

Nippon Origami Association, http://www.origami-noa.com

Toshiyuki, Meguro, http://www.geocities.co.jp/HeartLand-Oak/5487/

Mouse	6" (15 cm) origami paper
Squirrel	6" (15 cm) origami paper (Ogawa washi)
Partitioned Box	10" (24 cm) double sided origami paper
Conch	6" (15 cm) special origami paper
Santa Claus	6" (15 cm) origami paper
Giraffe	6" (15 cm) origami paper
Elephant	6" (15 cm) origami paper
Orizuru Transformation	6" (15 cm) origami paper (Ogawa washi)
Snake	12" (30 cm) wrapping paper
Airplane	8" (20 cm) foil paper
Samurai Helmet	10" (24 cm) double sided origami paper
Wild Boar	10" (26 cm) kozo paper (Echizen)
Dolphin	7" (17.6 cm) origami paper
Human Figure	6" (15 cm) processed washi
Japanese Macaque	10" (26 cm) kozo paper (Echizen)
Tree	10" (26 cm) kozo paper (Echizen)
Hina Dolls	6" (15 cm) origami paper
Fujiyama Module	3"x3/2" (7.5x3.75 cm) origami paper
Tea-bag Reindeer	tea-bag envelope of Nitto
Connected Cranes, Kotobuki	
	10"x16" (25x40.45 cm) gampi paper (Karasuyama)

Hommage to Escher's Reptiles
Jun Maekawa, 1980, pen on paper

Gift Box	12" (30 cm) processed washi
Squid	6" (15 cm) clear origami paper
Papillon (Dog)	7" (17.6 cm) origami paper
Three-headed Crane	6" (15 cm) origami paper (Ogawa washi)
Standing Crane	10" (25 cm) gampi paper (Omi)
Cow	11" (28 cm) craft paper
Sheep	12" (30 cm) origami paper (Ogawa washi)
Western Dragon	24" (60 cm) wrapping paper
Horse	12" (30 cm) craft paper
Triceratops	13" (33 cm) wrapping paper
Rabbit	10" (24 cm) kozo paper (Echizen)
Tiger Mask	6" (15 cm) double sided origami paper
Devil Mask	12" (30 cm) origami paper (Ogawa washi)
Penguin	10" (24 cm) origami paper
Frog	6" (15 cm) origami paper
Pyramid	32" (80 cm) OK Sand

Original: Reptiles
M. C. Escher, 1943

Chick	6" (15 cm) origami paper (Ogawa washi)
Peacock	12" (30 cm) Pike 65 kg
Turkey	12" (30 cm) Karape
Tyrannosaurus	18" (45 cm) OK Golden River 70
Eastern Dragon	16" (40 cm) gampi paper (Omi)
Samurai Helmet Beetle	12" (30 cm) origami paper
Devil	18" (45 cm) S Vellum Color Ramie

Jun Maekawa was born in Tokyo in 1958.
He studied physics at Tokyo Metropolitan
University. He is the executive officer and engineer
at a scientific computation software company,
a pioneer of technical origami design using crease
patterns, a researcher on mathematics, science,
history, and ethnology of origami, and a collector of
items related to orizuru (origami crane).

He is now the president of Japan Origami
Academic Society. He taught origami in Brazil
appointed by the Japan Foundation in 1989, and
co-administered the second International Meeting
of Origami Science and Scientific Origami in 1994.

He is the author of *Viva! Origami* (edited by
Kunihiko Kasahara, Sanrio, 1983) and the co-
author of *Bi-no Zugaku* (Morikita Publishing, 1998),
Origami ^{3} (A. K. Peters, 2002), and other books.

ROSES, ORIGAMI & MATH

By Toshikazu Kawasaki

With an innovative and exciting approach to papercraft, Roses, Origami & Math streches this ancient art to the limits. Included in Roses, Origami & Math are instructions for creating the author's masterpiece, the Kawasaki Rose Series. Fully illustrated with clear, step-by-step instructions, this book is fun and filled with useful techniques for mathematics education and for the ambitious layman.

177 pp., 7 1/4✕10 1/8 in., 4 color photos, 173 b/w pages, hardcover.
ISBN 978-4-88996-184-3

US $ 25.00

UNIT POLYHEDRON ORIGAMI

By Tomoko Fuse

Simple instructions for crafting intricate, multi-part origami structures, without glue or tape. With step-by-step diagrams, detailed instructions and over 70 photogarapys in vibrant full-color, internationally-renowned origamist and author Tomoku Fuse offers an innovative approach to origami based on assembling separate, multi-dimentional shapes into one structre.

96 pp., 8 1/4✕10 1/8 in., full color, paperback.
ISBN 978-4-88996-205-5

US $ 20.95

ORIGAMI RINGS & WREATHS

By Tomoko Fuse

One of the most prolific and bestselling authors in the filed now teaches readers how to create 28 different accessories and decorative wreaths using origami. In this book, Fuse provides instructions for 28 different projects including both jewelry (brooches and earrings) and decorative pieces like wall hangings. Fuse shows how the choice of paper and color can produce a wide variety of items, for example by using red and green papers, the crafter can make festive wreaths perfect for the holidays.

94 pp. 7 1/8✕9 1/8 in., 48 color & 46 b&w.
ISBN 978-4-88996-223-9

US $ 18.00